THIS BOOK BELONGS TO

_____

This book shares incredible stories that remind us of God's tremendous promises and encourage us to live a bold life of faith.

—**Steve Green**, president, Hobby Lobby Stores, Inc.;
founder & chairman of the board, the Museum of the Bible

As a prayer mobilizer, I love reading books on prayer. It is rare that I find one as practical as *31 Decrees of Blessing for Your Work Life* by my friend, Os Hillman. Praying through this book is a practical way to bring your work under the hand of God.

—**Dave Butts**, chairman, America's National Prayer Committee

Os Hillman has released another masterpiece! Somehow, he managed to distill decades of hard-won wisdom and remarkable stories into a 31-day devotional. It is sure to inspire while giving you practical, actionable steps to advance your career and your walk with the Lord. Every page inspired me, and I found myself reading the entire devotional in one sitting. It's that good!

—**Michael Q. Pink**, author, *Selling Among Wolves*

31 Decrees of Blessing for Your Work Life is a daily manifesto of sorts, full of one-day-at-a-time quick thoughts that will enliven your leadership, equip your mind, embolden you to take a stand, and encourage you in your complex, often tiring world of leading your firm. You will love diving into the practical decrees and learning how to activate them on mission-critical arenas of sales, profit, clients, employees, and, yes, even your enemies.

—**Greg Leith**, CEO, Convene Corporation

Many followers of Jesus desire to honor God through their business ventures and create a legacy of faithful significance. This 31-day journey through powerful truths, provocative declarations, and a myriad of fundamental resolutions every believer must make can help change the course of your marketplace experience.

—**Mike Sharrow**, CEO, The C12 Group

There is no better way to start your day than trusting in God's promises. In *31 Decrees of Blessing for Your Work Life*, Os Hillman has done a masterful job weaving in Scripture, stories, and practical action to help you powerfully live out your faith each day.

—**Larry Julian**, author, *God Is My CEO*

This outstanding book is soaked in Scripture and filled with faith-inspiring testimonies and life-altering declarations that can help us fulfill our assignment.

—**Dr. Joseph Mattera**, pastor, Resurrection Church;
director, United Coalition of Apostolic Leaders

God speaks to us through stories, nudging us out of our comfort zones to trust him for miracles, impact, and more love. These amazing true stories and decrees of blessing inspire us to stretch our faith so that we can be more active parts of God's miracles in our world.

—**Karen Covell**, producer & founding director, the Hollywood Prayer Network

Os's book is certainly "for such a time as this." God has stated in Job 22:28, "You will also declare a thing, And it will be established for you; So light will shine on your ways" (NKJV). Os Hillman has given us a masterful tool to fulfill this Scripture in so many ways. Read it. Use it. Decree it!

—**Franklin Santagate**, executive vice president marketing, Pure Flix

31 Decrees of Blessing for Your Work Life is an extraordinary work, rich with profound biblical promises, inspired testimonies, and practical applications. Any reader that intentionally and courageously believes God's promises and takes the steps of faith depicted in this book is assured a transformed family and work life, enriched and empowered with God's blessings.

—**Steve Fedyski**, CEO, Cloudburst Entertainment

Os delivers again! How many times have you read Scripture, heard sermons, and prayed, only to later feel stranded and powerless when a testing desert experience is front and center? By not only reading but also applying these covenant promises to any situation, believers may now live in a place of power, protection, and perseverance unlike any before.

—**Jason Brown**, chief marketing officer, Marketplace Chaplains

Os Hillman is transparent and powerful. This daily devotional is practical, tactical, factual, and biblical. It is going to change the way we all approach our workplaces. We finally have a tool that will bring the power of God to work with us.

—**Jim Brangenberg**, radio host, iWork4Him

Os brings us a practical and inspirational brand of devotion, born of years in the workforce prior to full-time ministry. It's the kind of devotion where we live, where we struggle, where we hurt, and yet are urged on, pressing in and pressing higher. We are often not delivered from our troubles; Os helps us get closer to Jesus, who, alone, delivers us through our troubles.

—**Terry Botwick**, founder & president, Papatime

Os's book is terrific. I now see him as a spiritual pharmacist. What a great idea to create this easy reference source of these vital biblical declarations. It's a simple and powerful daily prescription for living a vigorously healthy spiritual life in Jesus, the Great Physician!

—**Gordon Pennington**, international advisor; mentor; branding and communications strategies consultant

God's Word brings us nearer to him as we read, ponder, profess, and practice it. Os Hillman's *31 Decrees of Blessing for Your Work Life* powerfully trains readers in the transformational lifestyle of not only believing but also declaring God's Word to bring focus to our faith and God's authority to every aspect of our lives.

—**Kathy Branzell**, president, National Day of Prayer Task Force

In this new book, Os challenges us to fully discover and actively apply God's covenant promises in the context of our work. The practical integration of God's living Word into our daily vocational challenges is a revelation and will inspire you to take bolder actions based on God's Word.

—**Karen A. Howells**, founder & president, The Howells Group; board member, 4 Word Advisory

You know all those books sitting on your shelf that promised you success and breakthrough but didn't deliver? This is not one of those. Solidly grounded in Scripture and faith, *31 Decrees of Blessing for Your Work Life* calls your spirit higher and trains you to use decrees to bring your work into alignment with heaven.

—**James Kramer**, CEO, Pneuma33 Creative and Commissioned

In *31 Decrees of Blessing for Your Work Life*, Os Hillman arms us with simple yet profound tools that, when engaged, have the power to shape the life that we long to experience. This is one of those books you buy by the case—every company retreat should be handing these out like candy!

—**Anna Kramer**, chief creative officer, Pneuma33 Creative and Commissioned

31 Decrees of Blessing for Your Work Life is another amazing way to get people in the workplace to pray daily, seek God, and continually shift their thinking about using their gifts in the workplace. Hillman helps people understand God's call on their lives to impact his kingdom every day, in every area in which they have influence.

—**Ford Taylor**, founder, TL Transformational Leadership / TL On Demand

In *31 Decrees of Blessing for Your Work Life*, Os Hillman gives practical and powerful insights to help us understand that our work is not just what we do, but it ultimately illumines who we are. Pick up this book and let these truths seep into your head and heart. Your view of your work will never be the same again!

—**Joe Battaglia**, broadcaster; producer; author, *The Politically Incorrect Jesus* and *Unfriended*

There is a global misunderstanding about the legitimate authority that workplace leaders have over their destiny and the destinies of their businesses. Os has compiled a testimony treasure trove of the lives of leaders who understood this authority and the responsibility that goes with it. But this book is not just a compilation of stories; it is also filled with the Scriptural evidence you can apply to your own life. *31 Decrees of Blessing for Your Work Life* is rich in wisdom and the breath of the Spirit!

—**Paul L. Cuny**, president, MarketPlace Leadership International; author, *Nehemiah People*

"You will also declare a thing, and it will be established for you; So light will shine on your ways."

JOB 22:28 NKJV

31 DECREES
OF
BLESSING

FOR YOUR
WORK LIFE

BroadStreet
PUBLISHING

CONTENTS

DEDICATED TO

PAMELA

*My helpmate and fellow lover of God's Word
who keeps the wind in my sail.*

FOREWORD

I first met Os Hillman at a meeting in Atlanta, Georgia, where he was the keynote speaker. I was at his book table buying every book he had ever written and, as Os tells the story, he "came over to see if I was friend or foe." I had never met him, but based on the profound wisdom from God's Word that I was seeing just skimming his marketplace books at that table, I was certainly hoping to be his friend. As the years have gone by, I have watched Os put that wisdom into practice in so many areas of his life. There are no walls or lines drawn between his workplace, worship, and personal life; God's Word and will flow freely through all of them with power and joy. I am grateful to be a friend and fan of Os. His daily TGIF devotions and marketplace books have challenged and changed the way we lead. *31 Decrees of Blessing for Your Work Life* will change the way you think and the way you live.

Our lives are filled with millions of thoughts. Have you ever stopped to think about the things you are thinking? Do you ask yourself, *Who told you that?* or *Where did you hear that?* Have you ever stopped to think about all the things you heard in one day? Do you ever pause to listen to what you are saying and then ask yourself, *Is what I am saying truth?* Do you ever stop and ask the following questions: *Are the words coming out of my mouth adding or taking away life? Are they helpful or hurtful? Do they declare God's truth, or are they coming from an opinion, preference, or emotion that I am feeling?*

If faith comes by hearing, what are you hearing, and how

is it shaping what you believe? Realize that our behavior follows our beliefs; it weakens or strengthens our lives based on how it aligns with what God says. Who are you listening to? Who are you believing and repeating? Are you ever at a loss for words—you don't know what to think or say? Our lives must be built on the solid rock of God's Word, will, and ways, not the shifting, often selfish opinions of the world around us.

Os' book is a practical way to put God's Word in front of ourselves every morning so that it fills our thoughts and shapes our day. Os has studied the Scriptures to bring God's wisdom and promises to our attention. This is not a random "name it, claim it" practice where you imagine what you want and attempt to claim it into reality. This is reality according to God, found in specific Scriptures that he has declared over his creation and his children, for his glory and purpose. Our assignment is to declare these in agreement with God in order to walk in God's authority and under God's authority. These declarations are God-authored, Spirit-inspired prayers of faith.

In 2 Timothy,

Kathy Branzell,

President, National Day of Prayer Task Force

INTRODUCTION

The Bible is a book of history, stories, and promises. It is an amazing collection of sixty-six books written over a period of fifteen hundred years by forty different authors. Someone counted the number of promises in the Bible and found around seventy-five hundred of them.

A covenant promise is a promise from God that we are to believe and pray into existence. Those promises can be for healing, prosperity, protection, security, peace, wisdom, and more. When Jesus prayed the Lord's Prayer that "heaven would come on earth as it is in heaven," that meant we were to pray and manifest his promises on the earth.

I've provided thirty-one categories of covenant promises for you to decree and claim for your work and life in this book. We will examine the various circumstances in Scripture and real-life stories of application of these verses to your daily work life. I'll share stories of those who are living out the Scripture.

When Jesus told his disciples that he was going to be leaving them, he said he was going to give them the keys of the kingdom to loose on earth and loose in heaven and bind on earth and bind in heaven. "And I will give you the keys of the kingdom of heaven, and whatever you bind on earth will be bound in heaven, and whatever you loose on earth will be loosed in heaven" (Matthew 16:19 NKJV).

Many examples in Scripture show people using their authority to decree a matter. They spoke things to be done and experienced the supernatural physical manifestation. Joshua spoke to the walls of Jericho to fall down, and they did. Jesus spoke to Lazarus to come forth, and he did. Jesus said to Peter to walk on the water, and he did.

All of these are examples of the Word being decreed over a matter. When God told Moses to "speak to the rock" instead of striking the rock, it represented a change in paradigm for Moses. God was calling Moses to operate at a new dimension he'd never experienced before.

Moving in a new dimension with God means moving in a greater dimension of faith. Sometimes *faith* is spelled *risk*. Peter risked drowning when Jesus invited him to walk on the water. The priests risked losing the ark of the covenant when crossing the Jordan River at flood stage. Joshua risked looking foolish by walking around the city of Jericho and blowing a trumpet to take a city in battle. There are many examples of faith requiring *risk*.

Most of us spend 70 percent of our waking hours at work. But few of us understand how to use the Word of God to help us succeed in our working life. We need help in knowing how to manifest God's presence in our work life. Moses said, "If your Presence does not go *with us*, do not bring us up from here" (Exodus 33:15 NKJV).

It's important to note that when we say we are to decree a thing, it does not mean that God is a genie who responds to every word we might decree. It must be combined with faith and the leading of the Holy Spirit in our lives. The church has been guilty of a name-it-claim-it heresy in the past that is not biblical. What we are talking about here is following what the Bible teaches about manifesting the Word of God in our everyday life and being led by the Holy Spirit. "The mature children of God are those who are moved by the impulses of the Holy Spirit" (Romans 8:14 TPT).

May this book allow you to enter a new dimension of faith as you decree the Word of God over your work, family, and everyday life.

I speak the glory of God over my work.

DAY ONE

SPEAK THE GLORY
OF GOD

*Put your heart and soul into every activity you do, as though
you are doing it for the Lord himself and not merely for others.*

COLOSSIANS 3:23 TPT

Stanley Tam might not be a household name, but his story epitomizes what we need to understand about our work life call—we are called to glorify and worship God through our work life.

Stanley Tam founded US Plastic Corporation in 1956. His company manufactures and supplies commercial and industrial plastic products to customers across the country. In 1955, he made an extraordinary decision. Following an urging he felt in prayer, he turned his entire business over to the Lord by forming a foundation to take 100 percent ownership of the company. The foundation distributes the profits from US Plastic Corporation to support communities and build churches across the world.

This desire to work for the Lord did not come out of nowhere. For years before the founding of USPC, this prayerful man felt the call to save souls for the Lord. It didn't make sense to those around him, and even Stanley wondered why God would send a businessman into the world to evangelize. However, in 1952, he went with an evangelist on a missionary trip in Korea. When an emergency forced the evangelist to return home, Stanley found himself standing in front of a crowd giving his testimony through an interpreter. As terrifying as the moment was for Dr. Tam, he later saw it as "one of the greatest experiences of my life."

Stanley's plant in Lima, Ohio, now covers five acres and faces Interstate 75, a major corridor through the state. If you pass the USPC plant, you won't miss it because the words *Christ is the answer* are visible day and night from the side of the building. Another sign of how Stanley Tam has acknowledged God as Lord of all that he does.

The business Stanley built, in which he does not own a single share, has generated over $140 million toward building God's kingdom here on earth. A humble man, Dr. Tam sees the act of legally turning his business over to God as merely a way to demonstrate his gratitude and obedience.[1]

But this is a powerful example of what you can accomplish when God is first in your life. Stanley Tam was not content to make God his partner. God is Stanley's boss, his employer, and every success USPC experiences belongs to God and for his glory. Today, realize that all that you own is God's. Our work is meant to worship God because our inheritance is tied to the work we do every day.

DECREES

I DECREE THAT:

1. My work is worship to God and done for the glory of God.

2. If I work my land, I will have plenty of bread, but if I follow worthless pursuits, I will lack sense.

3. Slothfulness will cast me into a deep sleep, and if I become an idle person, then I will suffer hunger. I will do neither.

4. In all my toil there is profit, but mere talk leads only to poverty. I will have profit from my toil.

5. Whatever I put my hand to, I will do with all my might to ensure success.

6. If I'm not willing to work, I will not eat. I will not walk in idleness.

7. The favor of the Lord shall be upon me; the Lord will establish the work of my hands.

8. I will trust in the Lord with all my heart and not lean on my own understanding. I will acknowledge God in all my ways so that he will make straight my paths.

9. When I commit my work to the Lord, my plans will be established.

10. I will not be anxious about tomorrow, for tomorrow will be anxious for itself. I trust God as my provider.

Decrees based on the following Scriptures: Colossians 3:23;
Proverbs 10:4; Proverbs 12:11; Proverbs 14:23; Proverbs 19:15;
2 Thessalonians 3:10; Psalm 90:17; Proverbs 3:5,6; Proverbs 16:3;
Matthew 6:34

ACTIVATION

As we begin these thirty-one days of decrees, we must settle the ownership question. God bought each of us with a price, the death of Jesus Christ. He paid our debt of sin. When we commit our lives to Jesus, we commit every aspect of our lives, including our work life. God is all about work. He created the entire world. He gave Adam and Eve a world to steward. He gave each of us a unique DNA, giving us different talents and abilities, in order to serve the needs of others. Today commit not only your personal life to Jesus but also your work life. If you are a business owner, give your business to the Lord, for he is a great steward of what is his. Become God's manager.

Consider praying this prayer. If you are not ready to pray this prayer, come back to it when you are ready.

Father, I thank you for saving me. I receive Jesus as Lord of my life and my work. I desire to manifest your presence in all that I do. May you be glorified through the work of my hands so that I might receive my inheritance from the work you have called me to do. In Jesus' name, amen.

DAY TWO

SPEAK TO YOUR MOUNTAIN

Jesus replied, "Let the faith of God be in you. Listen to the truth I speak to you: If someone says to this mountain with great faith and having no doubt, 'Mountain, be lifted up and thrown into the midst of the sea,' and believes that what he says will happen, it will be done."

MARK 11:22–23 TPT

Does God do miracles in business? Is he concerned about the mountains we face in our life? Does he want us to bring the everyday problems we face in the workplace to his attention? The answer to every one of these questions is yes. God wants to be involved in every aspect of our lives.

Gunnar Olson, the Swedish founder of the International Christian Chamber of Commerce, tells a story about God performing a miracle in his own business several years ago. He was founder of a plastics company in Sweden. They made huge plastic bags that were used to cover bales of hay in the farmlands across Europe. It was the harvest season, and they were getting ready to ship thousands of pallets of these bags to their customers. More than one thousand pallets were ready to ship when they made an alarming discovery. Every bag on the warehouse floor had sealed shut from top to bottom. Scientists declared the entire stock as worthless trash. Nothing could be done. The company would go out of business.

Gunnar, his wife, and children sought the Lord in prayer about this catastrophe. The Holy Spirit spoke through various family members. Gunnar's wife said, "If God can turn water into wine, what are plastics?" His daughter said, "I don't believe this is from the Lord. We should stand against it." Gunnar sensed they were to trust God for a miracle in this situation. They began to pray. They took authority over this mountain of a problem based on Mark 11, which gave them the authority to cast a mountain into the sea if faith only the size of a mustard seed could be exercised.

On Sunday night, Gunnar stood outside his plant and said, "Listen heaven, listen earth, who is the Lord over Alphapac? It's Jesus. I now command all the bags to rotate back to their original place!" He and his family went inside the warehouse and laid hands on every pallet, asking the Lord to restore the bags to their original condition. It took several hours. On Monday, the employees began to inspect the bags again. As they inspected the bags, they discovered that every single bag had been restored to its original condition! An incredible miracle had taken place. The inspectors who discovered the original problem returned to validate that a miracle had taken place.

Do you need a miracle in your life today?

DECREES

I DECREE THAT:

1. I am a steward of all that God entrusts to me.
2. I will perform my work as a faithful steward.
3. I willingly lay down my life and work to God.
4. I will overcome every obstacle through the power of Christ.
5. God will bless all that I put my hand to.
6. I forgive all who wrong me so God's blessing can freely flow to me.
7. I am born to overcome the world through faith.
8. Just as the cattle on a thousand hills are God's, I, too, am entrusting all that I have to God.
9. I was bought with a price through the death and resurrection of Jesus Christ. I proclaim that I am his and his alone.
10. The blessing of the Lord will bless my life without sorrow.

Decrees based on the following Scriptures: Psalm 50:10–12; 1 Corinthians 6:20; John 15:13–16; Proverbs 10:22–24; Genesis 1:28; Jeremiah 1:19; Isaiah 57:14

ACTIVATION

What obstacles have been placed in your life that need a miracle today? Could God be setting the stage in your life for you to trust him at new levels you've never trusted before? God sets the stage to reveal his power for those willing to exercise the faith of a mustard seed. All things are possible with God. Speak to the mountain in your life today and proclaim God's blessing over it. Write out your decree.

_____

_____

_____

_____

_____

_____

_____

_____

_____

_____

_____

_____

_____

SPEAK PROVISION FOR THE NEEDY

Then she left, and went and gleaned in the field after the reapers. And she happened to come to the part of the field belonging to Boaz, who was of the family of Elimelech.
RUTH 2:3 NKJV

What is the purpose of a Christian-owned business? There isn't just one purpose. One purpose is to provide a living for those who work in the business. Another is to be a Christian witness to employees, vendors, and clients. Another is to fund Christian enterprises. And another is to care for the poor.

This last purpose for a business, caring for the poor, is rarely talked about in Christianity. This concept was understood in the Old Testament. Boaz was a successful farmer. He understood that part of his responsibility to his community was to allow the poor to come and glean from his field after he had harvested the main crop. While the harvesting was happening, widows, the poor, sojourners, and orphans all had the right to go into the fields behind the harvesters to pick up any leftover grain.

This was their version of welfare for the poor. No food stamps. No handouts. You actually had to do something to put food on your table. But it was in cooperation with businesses and farms in their area.

Life had hit Naomi and her daughter-in-law Ruth really hard. Both had lost their husbands and were having a tough time. They were unemployed and wondering where their next meal was going to come from. They picked up all their belongings and moved to Bethlehem during the barley harvest time.

There is a bigger picture to the story of Ruth and Naomi. God uses the business owner Boaz to fulfill the purposes of God. You see, as a relative of Elimelek, Naomi's deceased husband, Boaz had the ability to take Ruth, Naomi's daughter-in-law, as his wife. So this wasn't just any field. It was a field of hope and a solution to her plight. Ruth did all she knew to do, but God orchestrated events that would lead to her marriage to Boaz and being the seed that would lead to lineage of David and the Messiah—all this from a business!

The Bible tells us in Deuteronomy 8:18 that God gives us the ability to create wealth to establish his kingdom on earth. That is a core purpose of a Christian-owned business. It's also part of our purpose as believers in the workplace. Whatever we earn, a portion of that money should be directed at helping the poor.

There are many verses that tell us we are to care for the poor in our midst. Today, consider how you will help the poor as part of the fruit of your work life calling.

DECREES

I DECREE THAT:

1. I will be gracious to the poor because God says when I do this, I lend to the Lord, and he will repay me for my generosity.
2. I am blessed because I consider the helpless; the Lord will deliver me in my day of trouble.
3. When I give to the poor, I do not let my left hand know what my right hand is doing. I do this in secret.
4. If I shut my ear to the cry of the poor, I will also cry myself, and God will not answer my prayers.
5. When I give to the poor, I will never want, and if I shut my eyes to the poor, I will have many curses.
6. I will vindicate the weak and fatherless; I will do justice to the afflicted and destitute.
7. I will be a person who seeks justice, reproves the ruthless, defends the orphan, and pleads for the widow.
8. I will give of my possessions to feed the poor, and I will love my neighbor as myself.
9. I will care for widows and orphans as proof that I am a follower of Jesus.
10. I will be a father to the fatherless and defender for widows.

Decrees based on the following Scriptures: Deuteronomy 8:18; Leviticus 19:9–10; Deuteronomy 24:19; Proverbs 19:17; Psalm 41:1; Matthew 6:3; Proverbs 21:13; Proverbs 28:27; Psalm 82:3; Isaiah 1:17; 1 Corinthians 13:3; Mark 12:31; James 1:27; Psalm 68:5

ACTIVATION

We see the heart of God in the many Bible passages that talk about the poor. Many throughout the world live in poverty. Many Christian organizations serve the poor. Today consider how your business or work life call can be a catalyst to care for the poor. You'll be touching God's heart and know you are in the will of God for your generosity.

_____

_____

_____

_____

_____

_____

_____

_____

_____

_____

_____

_____

_____

_____

DAY FOUR

SPEAK TO YOUR SALES

Jesus replied, "Let the faith of God be in you. Listen to the
truth I speak to you: If someone says to this mountain with
great faith and having no doubt, 'Mountain, be lifted up and
thrown into the midst of the sea,' and believes that what he
says will happen, it will be done."

MARK 11:22–23 TPT

My first book, *TGIF: Today God Is First*, was published in 2000. Because I was a new author, the publisher required me to agree to purchase one thousand copies of the book. The internet was really just getting going at that time, and my ministry was beginning to grow. However, I was not selling many books in the beginning. In fact, I was not selling more than three or four copies a week.

I felt burdened because I was not selling more books. One Saturday morning, I awakened and had a strange instruction I believe was from the Lord. What I heard in my spirit was, *Go down to your basement and speak to your mountain of books and tell them to leave*. What a strange word. It brought back to mind what Gunnar Olson did with his plastic bags years earlier. He decreed that his broken bags would be unsealed. And they were!

I went downstairs and laid my hands on my mountain of boxes of books and said in a firm voice, "In the name of Jesus, I command you to get out of this basement and go be a blessing to someone who can use these books!" I must admit I felt a bit foolish.

Later that day around 2 p.m., I received a phone call. My office was closed, but since I operated from my home, I was there. A ministry in Dallas, Texas, called and said they would like to order three hundred copies of my book. It was a $3000 order!

I was shocked and rejoiced in how God led me to decree a thing and it actually happened the same day. What a boost to my faith!

DECREES

I DECREE THAT:

1. When I plant seed in the ground, God will bless that seed and cause it to multiply and prosper.
2. God will open his good treasure to me, give rain to my land, and prosper the work of my hands.
3. I shall lend to many nations and not borrow.
4. I shall open new markets that were previously devastated.
5. I shall create wealth to fulfill God's covenant promise to me.
6. I will prosper in all things and be in health.
7. I will be generous because those who water others shall be watered themselves.
8. I will multiply what is already in my hand.
9. I will receive downloads of witty inventions that will solve problems.
10. I will achieve through God's power above and beyond what I can imagine or think.

Decrees based on the following Scriptures: Psalm 107:37–38;
Deuteronomy 28:12; Isaiah 61:4; Deuteronomy 8:18;
3 John 2; Proverbs 11:25; 2 Kings 4:2; Proverbs 8:12;
Ephesians 3:20; Ephesians 2:10

ACTIVATION

Every business has a product or service it must sell. There are often times when sales become stagnate—a recession, a product malfunction, or a change in the market could affect sales. For many reasons, we might experience a lack of resources due to outside circumstances. God's economy is never without a solution to these times. It is up to us to seek God's solution for any downturn. God is always looking to demonstrate his power in difficult circumstances. There is no problem for which God does not already have the solution. He is looking for us to partner with him in that solution. Today tell God about the circumstance that needs his power demonstrated. Do you need more sales? Do you need to motivate your team? Do you need another income source? God said, "If any of you lacks wisdom, let him ask of God, who gives to all liberally" (James 1:5 NKJV).

_____

_____

_____

_____

_____

_____

_____

_____

_____

_____

Day Five

Speak to Your Provision

Your maidservant has nothing in the house but a jar of oil.

2 Kings 4:2 NKJV

Her husband had died. There was no way to fulfill her debts. Her creditors decided to take her two sons as slaves for payment of the obligations that remained. She pleaded for assistance with the only man of God she knew.

"Is there anything in your house?" Elisha asked.

"Nothing at all," she said, "except a little oil."

Elisha then instructed her to go and collect all the empty jars that her neighbors might possess. "Ask for as many as you can," he instructed.

When the jars were collected, he instructed her to pour what little oil she had into the jars. The oil was more than enough to fill the jars. In fact, there was more oil than jars to fill. God supernaturally filled every oil lamp. "Go, sell the oil and pay your debt; and you *and* your sons live on the rest. (2 Kings 4:7 NKJV).

God often mixes faith with the tangible. The widow believed she had no resources to meet her need. God said she had more than enough resources. She did not see the one jar of oil as a resource. It did not become a resource until it was mixed with faith. Her need was met when her faith was mixed with the practical step of going into the workplace to sell what she had in order to receive her needed income. In fact, there was so much income she was able to pay her debts and live on the money derived from the sale.

Quite often, we forget that God works through commerce to provide for our needs. But sometimes we must combine commerce with faith. It is wrong to place total trust in commerce without faith in God. God often requires simple obedience to an act that seems ridiculous to the logical mind. It is this faith mixed with the practical that God honors.

What do you have in your hand that God can multiply?

DECREES

I DECREE THAT:

1. I will have all I need each day because my God promises to provide for every need that I have through his riches in Christ Jesus.
2. I will use what I have in my hand to multiply my provision needed daily.
3. I will trust God to give me witty inventions.
4. I will refuse to lean on my own understanding but acknowledge God so he can direct me in all my ways.
5. I will abound in every good work God has entrusted to me.
6. God is Jehovah-Jireh, my provider, in all things.
7. No weapon formed against me shall prosper.
8. God shall make all grace abound toward me in all my endeavors.
9. I will always have all sufficiency in all things and may have abundance for every good work.
10. Wherever I go, I will have favor.

Decrees based on the following Scriptures: Philippians 4:19; 2 Kings 4; Exodus 16:21; Proverbs 3:5–6; 2 Corinthians 9:8; Isaiah 54:17; Psalms 5:12

ACTIVATION

Do you have a problem that is perplexing to you? Do you see no way of meeting your need? God may have already given you the skills and talents to meet your need. However, he may be waiting for you to mix them with faith. Ask God to show you the steps necessary to solve your problem. Be willing to take the next step.

_____

_____

_____

_____

_____

_____

_____

_____

_____

_____

_____

_____

_____

_____

_____

DAY SIX

SPEAK TO YOUR CIRCUMSTANCE

The people shouted when the priests blew the trumpets.
And it happened when the people heard the sound of the
trumpet, and the people shouted with a great shout,
that the wall fell down flat.

JOSHUA 6:20 NKJV

The Bible holds some remarkable stories. When Joshua and Caleb entered the promised land with a whole new generation of people, God said they were to destroy their enemies. They would fight thirty-nine battles in their quest for a new land where Israel would live. Their first battle was at Jericho. But instead of preparing for battle like most armies, God told them to do several strange things. Jericho had walls that their weapons could not penetrate. God said he had already given them Jericho; they just had to take it. But how? Here were the instructions:

He and his men were to walk around Jericho one time.

They were to do this for six days.

Seven priests would bear seven trumpets of ram's horns before the Ark of the Covenant.

On the seventh day, they were to walk around the city seven times and then blow the trumpets.

On the seventh blow, Joshua and his men were to shout.

Upon this shout, the walls would fall down!

I have often pictured this ridiculous scene. Imagine what the generals of his army must have thought. *Joshua has lost his mind. Are you saying we are not going to have to scale the wall?—let's get real, Joshua! God doesn't work that way!* I am sure some wanted to defect by this time, but that is not recorded in the story.

Faith sometimes appears as foolishness to onlookers. God asks us to do strange things to see if we are going to be obedient.

When I was dating my wife, there was a period where she had to move from her current home to another home before we got married. She had five dogs. It was not easy finding a rental home that would allow five dogs. We finally found a home that was just right and accepted her dogs. We placed an offer on the house. We were going to meet at the house that day for a second look. The owner of the rental company happened to be a former client of mine. I called him and made our offer. He put me on hold and said, "Os, you will need to hunt for another property. This one has been contracted by an executive from Apple. His credit is good, and that is normally what will disqualify someone."

I called my fiancé and told her the bad news. "I guess we don't need to go to the house now," I said.

"No! That is my house! We need to go to the house and walk around it and claim it."

"Are you sure, honey?" I said.

"Yes, that is our house!" We went to the house, walked around it, and claimed it for my wife, just like Joshua walked around the city. We canceled the contract in prayer.

A few hours later, I got a phone call from the owner of the business. He said, "Os, I have no idea what happened to this contract; the client has changed his mind. The house is yours if you still want it."

I had to repent for my lack of faith.

DECREES

I DECREE THAT:

1. God will bless me abundantly so that in all things at all times, having all that I need, I will abound in every good work.

2. God has made me strong and of good courage to overcome all obstacles and circumstances.

3. I will prosper because I will not turn to the right or left, but I will keep my focus on God. All my circumstances will work together for good.

4. I will meditate on your law both day and night so that I will be prosperous and have success in my work and life. Difficult circumstances allow God and me to solve problems together.

5. I will be courageous and not afraid because God has promised to be with me wherever I go. I will see negative circumstances as my opportunity for growth.

6. I am able to do immeasurably more than I ask or imagine, according to God's power that is at work within me.

7. I will operate in faith, believing that my faith is the substance of things hoped for, the evidence of things not seen.

8. Whatever I ask in prayer, I will receive if I have faith.

9. My faith will not rest in men's wisdom but in the power of God.

10. Nothing is impossible with God. I will see all circumstances as an opportunity.

Decrees based on the following Scriptures: 2 Corinthians 9:8;
Joshua 1:3–9; Hebrews 11:1; Matthew 21:22; Luke 1:37;
1 Corinthians 2:4–5; Romans 8:28

ACTIVATION

Living a life of faith and not doubting is the demarcation line of a healthy and exciting life with Christ. If we are not experiencing the life of God in all we do evidenced by answered prayer and miracles, we are simply living a life of religion. In Acts 5, we see the lifestyle of the apostles and those who witnessed faith in their lives. Notice their reactions to the apostles' lives. "And through the hands of the apostles many signs and wonders were done among the people. And they were all with one accord in Solomon's Porch. Yet none of the rest dared join them, but the people esteemed them highly" (Acts 5:12–13 NKJV). The people admired the apostles at a distance, but they did not join them. These were spectators of the activity of God. Today commit yourself not to be a spectator of God's activity in others. Paul said his preaching was not with wise and persuasive words but a demonstration of the power of God working through him (1 Corinthians 2:4). Ask God to move in your life so that you can see his activity in and through your life.

_____

_____

_____

_____

_____

_____

_____

_____

DAY SEVEN

SPEAK WORDS OF LIFE

Your words are so powerful that they will kill or give life,
and the talkative person will reap the consequences.

PROVERBS 18:21 TPT

The Bible speaks a great deal about the power of our words. When you speak positive words to your children, they will produce positive effects upon them. However, if you shame those around you and tell people they are no good or will never amount to anything, that, too, will have an effect on them. Many adults can remember times in their life when their parents spoke negative words to them.

Ted Turner, founder of CNN, recalls when his father used to tell him he would never amount to anything. His father spoke negative words to him all throughout his childhood. When he became an adult, he decided he would work hard to prove those words were not true. He became so bonded to those words that he had to succeed at all cost because if he didn't, his father's words would be fulfilled.

Some scientists even speculate that human words can transform the molecular structure of water. Dr. Masaru Emoto, a Japanese scientist and secular researcher, hypothesized that water took more beautiful, aesthetically pleasing crystalized forms when exposed to the love and compassion of humans. On the other hand, molecules of water in the presence of negative intentions became disfigured and ugly.

Dr. Emoto's controversial experiments involved labeling

some bottles of water with positive messages—such as love, peace, and gratitude—and others with negative messages—such as evil, fear, and disgust. The molecules of the water with the positive messages formed into shapes like bright diamonds when Emoto froze and photographed them. The other water molecules turned yellow, became disconnected and distorted.

He concluded that the vibrations of certain words and their intentions can have a transformative effect on the molecular structure of water. Doesn't it make sense that positive or negative words can have just as profound an effect on us?[2]

Let your words give life, not death.

DECREES

I DECREE THAT:

1. My tongue has the power of life and death; I will eat the fruit of my words which will give life, not death.
2. My mouth speaks what my heart is full of, so I choose life and blessing.
3. I will speak only wholesome words that build up according to the needs that exist.
4. I will speak words that give life instead of empty words that will be judged.
5. I will be a person who is quick to listen, slow to speak, and slow to become angry.
6. I will be a person who finds joy in giving an apt reply that is a timely word.
7. My word will go out from my mouth and will not return to me empty but will accomplish what I desire and achieve the purpose for which I sent it.
8. I will be accountable to all my words, for God will use my words to justify or condemn me.
9. My conversation will always be full of grace and seasoned with salt so that I may know how to answer everyone.
10. My words reveal the abundance of my heart, so I will speak words to give life and build up those around me.

Decrees based on the following Scriptures: Proverbs 18:21; Ephesians 4:29; Matthew 12:26; James 1:19; Proverbs 15:23; Isaiah 55:11; Matthew 12:34–36; Romans 8:31–32

ACTIVATION

What words have been used in your life to give life or death? Today you must cancel all word curses placed over your life. If a parent said, "You will never amount to anything," cancel those words with your audible words. Meditate on the decrees today and make them your prayer. Be a person who gives life through your words. Be an encourager. Voice those words; don't just think them. When you proclaim truth audibly, the brain hears these words. They are imprinted on the brain. Let God renew your mind according to the way he sees you. He is your greatest cheerleader.

"So, what does all this mean? If God has determined to stand with us, tell me, who then could ever stand against us? For God has proved his love by giving us his greatest treasure, the gift of his Son. And since God freely offered him up as the sacrifice for us all, he certainly won't withhold from us anything else he has to give" (Romans 8:31–32 TPT).

_____

_____

_____

_____

_____

_____

_____

_____

_____

_____

SPEAK PEACE AND UNITY TO YOUR TEAM

I pray for them all to be joined together as one
even as you and I, Father, are joined together as one.
I pray for them to become one with us.

JOHN 17:21 TPT

William Wilberforce has one of the greatest leadership stories of all time. He accomplished great things for God and his country because of a commitment to work with about eighteen other individuals who made up the Clapham Sect, named after a city in England where Wilberforce and his friends lived.

William was born into the English aristocracy in 1759. His family was wealthy. His uncle and aunt exposed him to the gospel as a young man. He gave his life to Christ at age 28. He began to grow into maturity and began to have thoughts of being a minister. However, one of his mentors at that time was a man named John Newton. He was a converted slave trader who wrote the famous hymn "Amazing Grace." When William expressed his interest in pursuing the priesthood, Newton challenged him to stay in politics: "God has raised you up for the good of the church and the good of the nation, maintain your friendship with Pitt, continue in Parliament, who knows that but for such a time as this God has brought you into public life and has a purpose for you."[3] William took his advice and stayed in politics. He is credited for abolishing slavery in England after more than thirty years of work.

The Clapham group fellowshipped together regularly, ate together, went to church together, and generally did life together. They would ultimately use their combined time, talent, and treasure to achieve sixty-nine world-changing initiatives that impacted the social ills of England.

Jesus spoke often of the power of working together as a unified force. He said the key to more people believing in him as the Messiah was his body working together in a unified way. Similarly, moving in a unified effort in the workplace will produce incredible results. The people at Babel were working together and could not be stopped, so God had to separate them because they had the wrong motive for their unified effort. "And the Lord said, 'Indeed the people are one and they all have one language, and this is what they begin to do; now nothing that they propose to do will be withheld from them'" (Genesis 11:6 NKJV).

Building a unified team at work or in mission will yield incredible results when done with the right motive.

DECREES

I DECREE THAT:

1. I will make sure my team understands our vision and the purpose of our mission.
2. I will be a humble team player and share my time, talent, and treasure to allow God to use me for his purposes.
3. I will share my opinions and ideas with humility.
4. I acknowledge that as one person, I will chase a thousand, but with two people, I can put ten thousand to flight.
5. I will always offer a helping hand to ensure my team has the potential for the greatest success.
6. I will strive to be a servant leader my team can trust and respect.
7. I will be a godly relational leader that seeks the good of the team at all times.
8. I will make time for fellowship and fun along the way.
9. I will help others on my team to understand our unique strengths and weaknesses and leverage our strengths while reducing our weaknesses.
10. I will embrace diversity in thought and personality to insure I have a unique perspective to our endeavors.

Decrees based on the following Scriptures: Deuteronomy 32:30; John 17: 21–23; Titus 1:7–9; 1 Peter 5:5; Mark 10:42–45; Philippians 2:4; Proverb 15:2; 1 Corinthians 12:7; Leviticus 26:8

ACTIVATION

God is all about working in teams. Consider Jesus, the Father, and the Holy Spirit as well as Jesus and the twelve disciples. He spent three years building a unified team. He understood a powerful team could accomplish so much more than one person. However, great teams don't just happen. It requires the leader to build godly attributes into the team and model servant leadership. Today ask yourself how you can be a better team player. How can you model the attributes listed above to make a powerful team, whether at work, home, or at church? List three things you need to do better to be God's team player and pray a decree over those three areas that you will walk in those attributes beginning today.

_____

_____

_____

_____

_____

_____

_____

_____

_____

_____

_____

_____

_____

_____

SPEAK FINANCIAL BLESSING

*You shall remember the LORD your God, for it is He who gives
you power to get wealth, that He may establish His covenant
which He swore to your fathers, as it is this day.*

DEUTERONOMY 8:18 NKJV

The Bible does not teach that every person who believes in
God will be financially prosperous. However, it does say that when
you combine the principles in Scripture with your skill, ability, and
favor of God, it results in a blessed life. It also says he has given you
abilities that can allow you to create wealth. Financial prosperity
is a by-product rather than a goal to achieve. Abraham, Isaac, and
Jacob were wealthy. David was wealthy. This came from their
obedience to God's call on their lives. Others were not so wealthy.

The above verse reveals to us that we each have the power
to generate wealth through our work life call. And the purpose
of that wealth is to establish God's kingdom on earth. Our wealth
should fund kingdom work so that the gospel will spread all
around the globe. The Bible tells us we can do all things through
Christ who strengthens us. We also know that Satan wants to steal,
kill, and destroy our lives. He does not want us to prosper. He does
not want us to give money to Christian causes. So, we need to
recognize we are in a spiritual battle.

A godly entrepreneur has the ability to see opportunities to
create products and services to better the world. The result is often

wealth creation. However, Satan attacks the entrepreneur in two ways: He will involve himself in too many projects that can lead to a fracturing of his time and resources. A second temptation is to live a consumptive lifestyle that is not generous towards others. To counter this, we must be workplace leaders who are led by the Spirit of God (Romans 8:14) and be a people who are generous with our time, talent, and treasure. This will insure we are operating from a consecrated life to the glory of God.

Solomon had a dream in which God offered him anything he wanted. Instead of asking for riches, Solomon asked for wisdom. The result was that he was given riches, wealth, and honor (2 Chronicles 1:12). It became the by-product of his wisdom.

Billionaire David Green, founder of Hobby Lobby, a chain of arts and crafts stores in the US, is a great example of maintaining this balance. David modeled what it means to see your business as a source of blessing for all who come in contact with it. He and his family decided to give their business to the Lord. They set up a legal structure that insured 50 percent of their profits would go toward Christian causes, and they limited the amount of money that would come to every family member. If the company is ever sold, this structure will remain for future owners.

DECREES

I DECREE THAT:

1. I will seek wisdom over riches to insure I fulfill all of God's purposes through my life.
2. I will make my mind and my skills available to God to work through for his glory.
3. I will be a good steward of all my resources to build his kingdom on earth.
4. I will partner with God to receive witty inventions that will solve problems.
5. I will glorify God in all that I do because I know that my inheritance is tied to fulfilling my work life call.
6. No weapon formed against me shall prosper to hinder me from success in my work life call.
7. I shall fulfill every purpose for which God created me.
8. God will instruct me in the way I should go.
9. God teaches me to profit and leads me in the way I should go.
10. God is the source of all my blessings and all my ability to create wealth. I will not become proud by forgetting the source of my success.

Decrees based on the following Scriptures: 3 John 1:2; Philippians 4:12; Proverbs 30:8; Proverbs 19:8; Romans 8:14; 2 Chronicles 1:12; James 3:17; James 1:5–6; Proverbs 8:11; Colossians 3:23; Isaiah 54:17; Psalm 20:4; Psalm 32:8; Isaiah 48:17; Deuteronomy 8:11–18

ACTIVATION

God loves business. He loves to bless the work of our hands. He loves to give us witty inventions to solve problems. Our prayer today is to ask God to manifest his life and presence in what we do for a living. Ask God to reveal himself in what you do. Ask him to prosper the work of your hands. Today decree those things that need to happen in your work life so that you can prosper in all that you do. He says our inheritance is tied to how well we fulfill our work life calling.

"Put your heart and soul into every activity you do, as though you are doing it for the Lord himself and not merely for others.

For we know that we will receive a reward, an inheritance from the Lord, as we serve the Lord Yahweh the Anointed One! A disciple will be repaid for what he has learned and followed for God pays no attention to the titles or prestige of men" (Colossians 3:23–25 TPT).

_____

_____

_____

_____

_____

_____

_____

_____

_____

_____

Speak to Marriages Represented in Your Workplace

A man is to leave his father and his mother and lovingly hold
to his wife, since the two have become joined as one flesh.
Marriage is the beautiful design of the Almighty, a great and
sacred mystery—meant to be a vivid example of Christ and
his church. So every married man should be gracious to his
wife just as he is gracious to himself. And every wife should be
tenderly devoted to her husband.

Ephesians 5:31–33 TPT

Marriage in the context of our work life calling is important to bringing balance and mutual support, especially since so many households have two parents working outside the home.

I always admired the marriage of Ronald and Nancy Reagan. They seemed to be able to maintain a genuine love and care for one another in the midst of demanding jobs as President of the United States and First Lady. *Time* magazine published a story on seven marriage lessons that we can learn from the Reagans' marriage[4]:

1. *Be each other's best friend.* They genuinely liked being with each other, and their children often recalled their times alone when sharing a meal in front of the TV. They felt these were their most enjoyable times.

2. *Always have each other's back.* Nancy was quick to come to the defense of President Reagan when the media or political enemies attacked him.

3. *Show respect for each other's opinions.* They genuinely valued each other's opinions and wanted their perspectives on situations that arose.

4. *Encourage one another's dreams.* They shared in what each other's dreams were and how they might achieve them together.

5. *Participate in each other's struggles.* There were many struggles in their lives. Most noteworthy was when President Reagan got Alzheimer's. Nancy cared for her husband for many years before his passing.

6. *Have fun together.* They often rode horses together on their ranch. They loved doing things that were fun together.

7. *Never give up on your partner.* No matter how tough the situation or great the challenge, they were committed to each other.

Marriage is a representation of Christ and the church. Jesus laid down his life for his bride. As such, husbands and wives are to do the same. We are called to love our spouses in good and bad times. The pressures of our working lives can disrupt our marriages and families if we allow it. Make a commitment to make your marriage a priority above all else.

DECREES

I DECREE THAT:

1. I will put my marriage above my work and maintain a balanced life, so my spouse and children do not suffer from my lack of involvement in their lives.
2. As a husband, I will love my wife as Christ loved the church.
3. As a wife, I will honor and respect my husband and allow him to lead our family.
4. I will model the importance of marriage in our workplace to be a testimony to my team.
5. I will be intentional about making time for me and my spouse to read the Bible together and pray together.
6. I will seek to foster a deeper friendship with my spouse by sharing our life together.
7. I will pray for my spouse daily. I will never leave nor forsake her or him.
8. I will be a good listener and take my spouse's input.
9. I will be intentional about meeting the needs of my spouse, creating time for each other.
10. I will forgive my spouse when he or she fails me and will not keep a record of wrongs.

Decrees based on the following Scriptures: Ephesians 5:21–23; Genesis 1:27–28; Ephesians 4:2; Colossians 3:14; Mark 10:9; 1 Corinthians 13; Proverbs 3:3–4; 1 Peter 4:8; Song of Solomon 4:8; Hebrews 10:24–25; Proverbs 31:10; Romans 12:10

ACTIVATION

This week spend time with your spouse. Express your appreciation for him or her. List the qualities you appreciate about him or her. If you do not pray regularly together, begin this today. Read the decrees out loud and then pray together. Read a devotional on marriage together each day. Be intentional about living out the decrees. Make them a priority.

DAY ELEVEN

SPEAK GOD'S PROTECTION

Because you have delighted in me as my great lover,
I will greatly protect you. I will set you in a high place,
safe and secure before my face. I will answer your cry for help
every time you pray, and you will find and feel my presence
even in your time of pressure and trouble.

PSALM 91:14–15 TPT

If anyone understands how quickly and dramatically life can change, it's Pam Rhodes. For years, Pam has been a chaplain for Billy Graham's Rapid Response Team, a specially trained corps of volunteer ministers who deploy to all parts of the world when tragedy strikes. They pray with the dying, comfort survivors, and bring the light of Christ to those in the dark days of suffering.

In May of 2011, Pam and the Rapid Response Team raced to Joplin, Missouri, where a massive tornado had shattered the tranquility of a Sunday afternoon, leaving widespread destruction and many casualties. Pam heard one story in particular that demonstrates the all-powerful presence of Almighty God even when things seem hopeless.

A woman named Cheryl told Pam that on that Sunday afternoon, she noticed signs that a storm was coming. However, there was something unusual about it. The leaves on the trees glistened, and the sky moved strangely. Cheryl had just picked up her two daughters who had been at a high school graduation party, and they were heading home. She was sure she could make it home before the storm hit, but she didn't realize she was driving her van straight into an enormous tornado that was rapidly gaining strength.

When the little family was less than a mile from home, the rain started to fall like hammers on Cheryl's van. Perhaps Cheryl had not heard the warning sirens or the emergency broadcasts. Perhaps, like many in Joplin, she had heard them so often before that she didn't pay any attention. But when Pam Rhodes retells Cheryl's story, she emphasizes the evidence that God had not abandoned Cheryl and her daughters to the storm.

Cheryl told Pam that she watched the clouds form into long white fingers reaching out of the sky. With the rain beating down so hard, as if she were in a car wash, she felt God urging her to pull over. When the wind tugged at the vehicle, Cheryl realized what was happening. She and her daughters were in grave danger.

Suddenly, the windows blew out of the van. You can imagine the panic as this terrified mother pushed her daughters down to the floor of the van and began to pray, begging God to save them.

If you have ever had an encounter with the living God, you understand how lifechanging it can be. However, in the moment, you may not recognize what is happening. Inside the battered van, Cheryl and her daughters felt a powerful force holding them down, shielding them from the deadly debris the storm flung at the vehicle. Then, silence.

As the vortex passed over them, Cheryl felt a strange peace that assured her things would be all right. She heard the Lord comforting her: *Your daughters are going to be safe.* Then the storm resumed with its rain and fury. The twister snatched up the van and slammed it down, leaving Cheryl and her daughters trapped inside the wreckage that was covered in debris and downed power lines.

However, the Lord had not abandoned her. A gentle voice from outside the van assured Cheryl she would be okay. Cheryl saw a man standing next to the van. He was not injured or dirtied by the storm, and his presence filled the woman with peace.

When Cheryl told Pam Rhodes her story, she described the man as an angel. He said, "You don't have to be afraid," and he gently helped them out of the van with injuries no more serious than a few scratches. Then he was gone. But he left behind a woman who now understands that God is with her always, no matter what tragedy comes her way.[5]

Cheryl's story was only one of many ways in which the hand of God intervened on that dark afternoon. Pam and her team ministered to thousands of survivors and counseled the loved ones of over 150 who died in the tremendous storm. It is natural to wonder why God protected and spared Cheryl while so many others died. Pam wonders this herself. But even when your life radically changes for the worse, God remains the same loving and merciful God who desires only for your good.

DECREES

I DECREE THAT:

1. I will fear not, for God is always with me.
2. I will abide in the shadow of the Almighty.
3. The Lord will rescue me from every evil deed.
4. No weapon fashioned against me will prosper.
5. Even though I walk through the valley of the shadow of death, I will fear no evil, for God is with me; his rod and his staff, they comfort me.
6. God is faithful to protect me from the evil one.
7. God will never leave me nor forsake me. He has made me strong and courageous.
8. I entrust my business, my work, to God who watches over all that concerns me.
9. The Lord will perfect that which concerns me.
10. The Lord will watch over my coming and my going, both now and forevermore.

Decrees based on the following Scriptures: Isaiah 41:10; Psalm 91:1–16; 2 Timothy 4:18; Isaiah 54:17; Psalm 23:1–6; 2 Thessalonians 3:3; Deuteronomy 31:6; Psalm 138:8; Psalm 121:8

ACTIVATION

Things can change in life so quickly. A downturn in the stock market can change our status at work. A recession can cause layoffs. A failed product can cause a downturn in sales. A traffic accident can change life forever. We are not immune to changes in our life and work. But there is one thing that is constant: God says he will never leave us or forsake us. No matter what circumstance might change, God will not change. He is with us even in the storms of life. Today cite out loud the decrees above as a statement of faith in God who promises to be with us in the good times and the bad, in good economies and bad, and even in our crisis moments. If you are a business owner, proclaim God's protection over your business today. If you are a worker, ask God's favor on the work of your hands.

Speak Favor with Your Clients and Customers

Lord, how wonderfully you bless the righteous.
Your favor wraps around each one
and covers them under your canopy of kindness and joy.
Psalm 5:12 tpt

Modeling what Jesus taught can aid in discovering and applying the primary attributes of a kingdom business. We can learn a great deal about what type of workplace environment we should have based on looking at Jesus in the New Testament. Whether you are a Christian business owner or a Christian who works in a secular workplace, you can foster a different kind of culture by understanding and applying what Jesus taught.

Years ago I was interviewed by *The New York Times* for an article they were doing on Christians in the workplace. They interviewed me three times. On the third interview, they asked me an interesting question. The editor called me and said, "Our staff had a question that they could not answer. Perhaps you could help us with it. What makes a Christian different than a non-Christian in the workplace?"

It was a great question that caused me to ponder the answer. I posed this question to the Lord and felt I received the following answer: there are four key attributes to being a Christian in the workplace.

First, we must do our work with excellence. The Bible describes Daniel and his friends as people who did their work ten times better than anyone else. Bezalel was chosen by God to design the ark of the covenant. It was said that Bezalel was filled "with the Spirit of God, in wisdom and understanding, in knowledge and all manner of workmanship" (Exodus 35:30–31 NKJV). The second attribute is integrity. David said in Psalm 51 that "God desires truth in the inward parts." The third attribute is servant leadership. Jesus said if you want to be great in God's kingdom, be a servant of all. The fourth attribute is miracles. Jesus said he gave us the keys of the kingdom to do greater works than he did.

Your employees, clients, and vendors see your witness in the workplace. It's important that we model these four attributes in order to bring glory to God through our work life call. Modeling the character of Christ will give us the favor of God among the various audiences we serve.

DECREES

I DECREE THAT:

1. My clients and customers will be blessed because of their relationship with me.
2. I will bring blessing to all who come in contact with me.
3. I will be a person of integrity in my life and work.
4. I will model servant leadership in my life and work.
5. I will do my work with excellence.
6. I will depend on God to give me witty inventions to build God's kingdom on earth.
7. I will live and experience a life of miracles because I have the keys of the kingdom given to me by Jesus to bind and loose on earth and in heaven.
8. I will humble myself in the sight of the Lord so that he will lift me up.
9. I will look for creative ways to bless my clients and customers and solve problems.
10. I will forgive and bless my clients and customers who say bad things about me.

Decrees based on the following Scriptures: Daniel 1:20; Exodus 31:1–10; Psalm 51; Matthew 16:19; Genesis 39:5; Mark 10:44; Acts 5:12; James 4:10

ACTIVATION

Every day we rub shoulders with co-workers, customers, and sometimes our vendors. These represent relationships that we can impact positively or negatively. God calls you and me to represent his kingdom values wherever we go. Ask God to help you model excellence, integrity, servant leadership, and miracles. Today take time to pray for your coworkers, your clients, and your vendors. Ask God to open doors for you to share Christ with them. Proclaim God's truth over their lives. Offer to pray with any customer or client who might be going through a difficult time.

DAY THIRTEEN

SPEAK FAVOR OVER YOUR ENEMIES

Love your enemy, bless the one who curses you, do something
wonderful for the one who hates you, and respond to the very
ones who persecute you by praying for them. For that will
reveal your identity as children of your heavenly Father.

MATTHEW 5:44–45 TPT

In my book, *The Joseph Calling*, I write about six stages that God takes a leader through to fulfill the larger story of his or her life. One of those stages is The Cross. We are all called to go to the cross and give our lives up for Jesus Christ. However, that sounds like a noble thing to do until you are asked to lay down your life for someone else despite circumstances that might involve pain and betrayal. I often talk about God's graduate level course of Christianity that requires a test that we must pass. We might be fully committed to Christ and willing to go to the cross, but even if we were willing, we could only put two nails in that cross. So often, God raises up a third person through a betrayal to put that third nail in our cross.

Betrayal is one of the most painful experiences a person can go through. Several figures in the Bible experienced betrayal. Moses's sister, brother, and Korah betrayed Moses. Joseph's brothers betrayed him. Judas betrayed Jesus. David's son betrayed him and struggled when a close friend betrayed him:

But it was you, my intimate friend—one like
a brother to me. It was you, my advisor, the
companion I walked with and worked with!
We once had sweet fellowship with each other. We worshiped in unity as one, celebrating
together with God's people. Now desolation
and darkness has come upon you. May you
and all those like you descend into the pit of
destruction! (Psalm 55:13–16 TPT)

Jesus said the only solution to a betrayal is forgiveness. Not
only does he tell us to forgive those who betray us, but he also
actually tells us to bless them. Jesus washed the feet of his betrayer.

This graduate level course is for leaders who want to be used
mightily in the kingdom of God. Forgiveness frees you to become
God's leader. It frees you from the prison of being a victim. It
demonstrates the unconditional love to the betrayer that they
may not deserve forgiveness, but you are offering it to them to
gain freedom for themselves. Jesus also added one more caveat to
his instruction:"By the way, if you don't forgive them, I will not
forgive you" (my paraphrase).

May you pass God's graduate level course today.

DECREES

I DECREE THAT:

1. I choose to forgive those who have betrayed me or wronged me.
2. I will actively bless those who have wronged me.
3. I recognize that God has forgiven me of my sins, which means there is nothing I cannot forgive because of his forgiveness of me.
4. I acknowledge the pain of my betrayer but choose to submit my pain to God to allow him to heal me.
5. I choose to pray for my betrayer.
6. I choose not to judge but release the burden and the offender to God.
7. I acknowledge that as I forgive my betrayer, God will forgive me.
8. God will answer my prayers because I have forgiven those who have wronged me.
9. I forgive myself for my contribution to the relationship breakdown.
10. I have been reconciled to God through the forgiveness of my sins.

Decrees based on the following Scriptures: Numbers 14:18; Luke 6:37; Luke 17:4; 1 John 1:9; 2 Corinthians 5:5–8, 10; Matthew 6:12, 14–15; Mark 11:25; Colossians 3:13; Ephesians 4:32; Colossians 1:21–23

ACTIVATION

Have you ever heard someone say, "Forgive him? Do you know what he did?" Extending forgiveness to someone who did a hurtful thing is hard. Corrie Ten Boom once met the man who tortured and killed her sister when she was in the German concentration camps. It created great pain to see this man. However, she knew the only way to get free was to forgive this man. She did it. Think of someone who has hurt you. Have you offered forgiveness? Today is the day to forgive that person. Ask for God's grace to forgive so you can be free to live again. Write down the person's name and pray a forgiveness prayer for him or her.

_____

_____

_____

_____

_____

_____

_____

_____

_____

_____

_____

SPEAK PROTECTION IN TIMES OF UNCERTAINTY

Though the fig tree may not blossom, nor fruit be on the vines;
Though the labor of the olive may fail, and the fields yield no
food; Though the flock may be cut off from the fold, and there
be no herd in the stalls—Yet I will rejoice in the Lord, I will joy
in the God of my salvation. The Lord God is my strength;
He will make my feet like deer's feet, and He will make
me walk on my high hills.

HABAKKUK 3:17–19 NKJV

At 34, John Kavanaugh was looking for answers. Like many young men, he had several promising and exciting opportunities to choose from in the life of ministry for which he was training. When given the opportunity to spend a year in prayer and discernment, he chose to spend three months of that time working alongside Mother Teresa and her Little Sisters of the Poor, ministering to the destitute in the streets of Calcutta.

During his time at "The House of the Dying," he had many profound conversations with the holy woman, and he sought her wisdom and guidance as he considered his future. Should he travel abroad and work with the poor, or should he return to America to teach philosophy at a university? Kavanaugh asked Mother Teresa to pray for him.

"What do you want me to pray for?" she asked. He explained the painful search he had undertaken, traveling thousands of miles to discover where God wanted to use him. "Pray that I have clarity," he told the little nun.

"No, I will not do that," she answered firmly. He asked her why, and she replied that clarity was what Kavanaugh was clinging to. He needed to let go of his desire for clarity.

Kavanaugh was surprised and told her that he had always assumed she had clarity. He wanted to be as certain of his mission as Mother Teresa seemed to be. This made the nun laugh, and she said with all humility, "I have never had clarity; what I have always had is trust. So, I will pray that you trust God."[6]

St. Augustine is believed to have once said, "Pray as though everything depended on God; act as though everything depended on you." There is a lot of truth to the facts that we are called to trust and that we are called to work hard. The problem lies in the uncertainty of life and how many factors can upset our lives without warning.

When things that we have depended upon are removed from our lives, we are forced to decide where we will place our trust. The prophet Habakkuk found himself in such a time. His resources had dried up. The farms were not producing. He was solely dependent on God. So, too, we often find ourselves in such circumstances. But God's Word tells us that he is Jehovah Jireh, my Provider. While God is the constant provider of all that we need, there are times when we must experience supernatural trust in God to be that provider. Today, we will decree God's promises to be our provider in times of want and uncertainty as well as in our everyday needs.

DECREES

I DECREE THAT:

1. My God shall supply all my needs according to his riches in Christ Jesus.

2. My God will care for my every need just as he cares for the birds of the field.

3. I will have the peace of God which surpasses all understanding that will guard my heart and mind in Christ Jesus.

4. God is my helper and will uphold my life.

5. God exists and rewards me when I seek him.

6. When I ask, it will be given to me; when I seek, I will find; when I knock, it will be opened to me.

7. The Lord is my shepherd; I shall not want.

8. The Lord is the stronghold of my life; I shall not be afraid.

9. I will seek first the kingdom of God and his righteousness, and all these things will be added to me.

10. God will make all grace abound to me so that I have all sufficiency in all things at all times, that I may abound in every good work.

Decrees based on the following Scriptures: Habakkuk 3:17-19; Proverbs 3:5–6; Philippians 4:19; Psalm 50:11; Matthew 6:26–31; Philippians 4:6–7; Psalm 54:4; Matthew 7:7; Psalm 27:1; Matthew 6:33; 2 Corinthians 9:8; Luke 12:24

ACTIVATION

You may be faced with uncertainty right now. Now is the time to affirm God as your Jehovah Jireh, your provider. Proclaim the truth that God is able to provide every need you have. Declare and decree God's provision over your life. Decree that resources will come from the north, south, east, and west for the specific need you have. Begin thanking him for your provision.

_____

_____

_____

_____

_____

_____

_____

_____

_____

_____

_____

_____

_____

_____

_____

Day Fifteen

Speak Innovation and New Ideas

The entire universe is standing on tiptoe, yearning to see the unveiling of God's glorious sons and daughters!
Romans 8:19 tpt

In 1977, Matthew McPherson was like most nineteen-year-olds in that he was wondering what to do with his life. However, he stood apart from many his age because he sought the answer in prayer. It wasn't enough for Matt to have a plan for the future; he wanted to be sure he was doing what God wanted him to do. So he prayed for guidance, and God answered.

Matt clearly heard the Lord say to him, *I am going to prosper you in business so you can be self-sufficient in ministry.* This answer excited Matt. He had a generous heart, and the idea of being a businessman who could give to others was perfect for him. His Father in heaven went even further to make Matt's future exciting by guiding him to start a business based on Matt's lifelong love of archery and his skill at making bows.

Although he had been building his own bows since he was a child, mostly because he couldn't afford to buy one, he was still searching for a design that would give him an edge, something that would make his business unique. Again, he heard God's voice telling him, *I know every answer to every problem in the world. If men would only ask me, I'd give them those answers.*

Obediently, Matt went to his knees and asked the Lord for

wisdom. *Lord, direct me in a way that's unique and novel so I can build the best bows in the world, and I'll honor you with my life.*

Not long after that, Matthew received a vision from the Lord for a design for a revolutionary new compound bow. He woke up in the night and saw the design on a piece of paper hanging in front of his face. He laughed at the Lord's sense of humor. "It wasn't just a white sheet of paper, but it was notebook paper hanging in my face."

Matt worked patiently on the project and waited for God's good timing. He sought some investors and started his own archery manufacturing business in 1985. The superior design he had received through divine inspiration proved to be a quiet, accurate, high-quality bow unlike any on the market. His business took off, and within five years, Matthews Inc. grew from a one-man business to an Inc. 500 company and is now the largest manufacturer of archery equipment in the world.

Matt McPherson and his wife, Sherry, are living proof that God keeps his promises. Because of their thriving business, which is dedicated to God's honor and glory, the McPherson's have the privilege of living the promise God made to Matt all those years ago: that he would be self-sufficient in ministry. Matt and Sherry travel the world spreading the gospel through their music ministry and their support of missions.

They realize this is a joyful way to live, and as time passes, their business and their ministry have become the same. Matthew understands that being a Christian businessman means being an example of integrity, creativity, excellence, and love to the business world and beyond.[7]

God is the God of creativity and innovation. The problem is many Christians don't believe God is interested in business. Just look at God's world and see how creative and innovative he is. There are millions of ideas yet to be birthed. Our job is to ask and receive what God wants to give to his children.

DECREES

I DECREE THAT:

1. God wants to reveal secret things in hidden places for me so that I might know him.
2. I will be God's vessel to reveal new ideas and solutions for problems that need to be solved.
3. I will tap into God's creativity and innovation for new business opportunities.
4. God will reveal secrets to me of things yet to come.
5. God promises to reveal mysteries to me as his child.
6. I shall receive downloads from God in night visions and dreams.
7. I will receive mysteries from the darkness and bring the things in deep darkness into light.
8. God will reveal the mystery of his will, according to his kind intention, which he purposed in himself.
9. God has granted to me to know the mysteries of the kingdom of heaven.
10. God will reveal to me things I do not know to do great and mighty things.

Decrees based on the following Scriptures: Isaiah 45:3;
Jeremiah 33:3; Daniel 2:28; Daniel 2:19; Job 12:22;
Ephesians 1:9; Matthew 13:11; Ephesians 3:3;
1 Corinthians 2:10

ACTIVATION

Sometimes an idea that comes from God seems like it arrives by accident. Such was the case for the inventor of the Post-It® note. In the 1970s, Arthur Fry worked at the 3M factory during the week and sang in the choir at his church on Sundays. Like many choir members at the time, he struggled with paper bookmarks that would slip out of the hymnals, losing his place. In 1974, Spencer Silver, a fellow researcher at the 3M company, was working on an adhesive that would stick to surfaces temporarily and not damage them. The company wasn't sure what to do with this invention, but Fry had an idea.

He experimented with the formula and finally came up with a bookmark design that had the light adhesive on one end and allowed the other end of the paper to extend from the book. The Post-it® note was born. Management at 3M wasn't sure how to promote the little notes, but within a few years, the product became one of the most popular stationery items on the market. Post-it® notes are now available in dozens of shapes, sizes, and colors and are sold in over 100 countries.[8]

What idea does God want to birth through you? Today open your mind to new ideas and new inventions that God might want to give you through dreams, visions, and thoughts. Begin to prepare your mind to receive from God by making these decrees today.

_____

_____

_____

_____

_____

_____

Day Sixteen

Speak Blessing over Families in Your Workplace

It is not good that man should be alone;
I will make him a helper comparable to him.

Genesis 2:18 NKJV

Families are the foundation of society. From the first day he created man, God recognized that it was not good for him to be alone. So he created a woman to be a "helper suitable for him" (Genesis 2:18 NASB). God poured his blessing upon the man and the woman and instructed them to, "be fruitful, and multiply, and replenish the earth" (Genesis 1:28 KJV). Even after Adam and Eve sinned through their disobedience, God did not relinquish his plans for families. He even assured Eve that the salvation of mankind would come through her seed (Genesis 3:15).[9]

According to sociologists, the family as an institution serves three vital purposes: For raising children, for building among its members a sense of individuality as well as a connection to each other, and for carrying on elements of culture from one generation to the next. As Christians, the family is the place to raise godly leaders in society and teach them to be the head and not the tail in society (Deuteronomy 28:13). It is also the place to reveal the love of God.

The family is under attack like never before today. Even

73

the foundation of marriage is under attack. No longer does our government constitute marriage as a union between a man and a woman but between two consenting adults. This assault on our families can destroy the foundations of our nation. We must be a catalyst to stand in the gap for healthy families and a restoration of families in our nation and world. If the foundation of families fails, society will crumble.

When a Christian family functions within the biblical ideal, each member will be committed to Christ and active in his service. God appointed specific roles for husbands, wives, and children, and when family members joyfully fulfill their roles, they are more likely to live in peace and harmony. On the other hand, when we step outside of God's loving design for families or fail to place Christ at the head of our homes, suffering and unhappiness are sure to follow.[10]

Healthy families are key to a healthy society and healthy businesses. When a family breaks up, it affects everyone involved—spouses, children, businesses, and communities. A broken family fractures all of these relationships and causes much pain in the process.

God is for healthy families. He wants to see his love, compassion, servanthood, and godliness reflected through his families. Today, we will decree the restoration of godly families in our nation.

DECREES

I DECREE THAT:

1. There will be a restoration of the family made up of husband and wife. Husbands and wives will fulfill their marital covenant vows to each other.
2. Businesses will value godly families and the biblical roles of husband and wife.
3. Husbands will love their wives as Christ loved the church and lay down their lives for their wives.
4. Wives will fulfill their biblical role of honoring their husbands and working together with their husbands as co-heirs of the grace of God.
5. We will stand against the schemes of the devil to steal, kill, and destroy our families.
6. When I train my children under godly values, they will not depart from them.
7. Fathers will bring up their children in the discipline and instruction of the Lord.
8. Children will obey their parents so that they might please the Lord.
9. Children are a heritage from the Lord that parents shall welcome and bless.
10. Christian parents shall procreate to nurture and raise godly children.

Decrees based on the following Scriptures: Ephesians 6:10; John 10:10; Genesis 1:28; Genesis 2:18, 21; Proverbs 22:6; Colossians 3:20; Psalm 127:3–5

ACTIVATION

Today we need to stand in the gap for our families. Society is trying to change the makeup of what God says is a family. "Woe to those who call evil good, and good evil; Who put darkness for light, and light for darkness; Who put bitter for sweet, and sweet for bitter!" (Isaiah 5:20 NKJV). The family is made up of husband and wife and children. Sexual distortion and identity confusion have replaced common sense. Today decree the restoration of godly families in our society. Pray that the lie of alternative sexual identity will be exposed. Pray for our families and our nation to uphold and protect godly families.

_____

_____

_____

_____

_____

_____

_____

_____

_____

_____

_____

_____

_____

_____

SPEAK PEACE OVER CONFLICTS AMONG TEAM MEMBERS

If your brother sins, go and show him his fault in private;
if he listens to you, you have won your brother.

MATTHEW 18:15 NASB

Conflicts between co-workers are not uncommon, but often they arise from misunderstandings or lack of communication. When author, speaker, and leadership consultant Michael G. Rogers started a new job early in his career, he was careful not to make quick judgments or assumptions about his co-workers or the department in which he worked. However, there was one person in his department who gave Michael the uneasy feeling that she did not like him.

Ingrid was a large, loud, and intimidating woman who was quick to share her knowledge and opinions on any topic, from politics to company policies. She frequently offered unsolicited information about department processes and just as eagerly shared the latest gossip. However, when it came to Michael, she was curt and aloof.

After about six months on the job, Michael realized that Ingrid was not talking to him at all. He wasn't sure what to do about it. He brought the uncomfortable situation to the attention of his manager, who advised him to discuss the matter frankly with Ingrid. Otherwise, he had no hope of resolving the conflict.

Ingrid already intimidated Michael, and he shied from a confrontation with her. But he knew his manager was right. So one afternoon when Ingrid was walking past Michael's cubicle, he invited her to meet privately with him in the conference room to discuss the friction between them. To Michael's surprise, Ingrid wasted no time getting to the conference room, where she enumerated the reasons why she didn't like him. He responded by telling Ingrid the things about her that bothered him. Michael felt it was a healthy conversation, and he thanked her for meeting with him and getting their disagreements off their chests. Ingrid shocked Michael by assuring him that their conversation changed nothing. Using her typically colorful language, she promised Michael that she intended to remain angry at him for the foreseeable future.

Nevertheless, within a few days, Ingrid was responsive, even friendly toward Michael. Before long, Michael began to feel that he had become Ingrid's favorite colleague. This congenial relationship lasted until the day when management promoted Michael to the position of supervisor over Ingrid. The woman soon put in her notice and left the company.[11]

Conflict in the workplace is inevitable. However, conflict does not have to end badly. The Bible has a great deal to say about how we handle conflict. Today we are going to decree the biblical truths we can apply to handling conflict.

DECREES

I DECREE THAT:

1. Whenever I have a difference of agreement with a friend, spouse, coworker, or customer, I will go to them first in private to share my concern and give them an opportunity to share his or her view.

2. I will humbly seek to resolve conflict outside the court system whenever possible, especially with other believers.

3. I will exhibit respect, patience, and kindness toward those with whom I disagree.

4. I will not return evil for evil.

5. I will give a gentle answer to turn away wrath.

6. I will be quick to hear, slow to speak, and slow to anger.

7. I will respect what is right in the sight of all men.

8. I proclaim that I am one of God's peacemakers, who is a son or daughter of God.

9. I will not fall short of the grace of God; no root of bitterness will spring up that causes trouble and defiles me and others.

10. Should my brother or sister not listen to me, I will take two or three with me to share my concern to have a matter established.

Decrees based on the following Scriptures: 1 Corinthians 14:4–7; James 1:19–20; Ephesians 4:29; 1 Peter 3:8–11; Matthew 5:38; Proverbs 15:1; Matthew 5:9; Matthew 18:15–17; 1 Corinthians 6:1–6; Hebrews 12:15

ACTIVATION

Is there a person with whom you have conflict in your workplace or life? God's Word gives us practical advice on handling conflict. Go to the person first in private. Share what you understand the conflict is about to allow them to confirm or correct your assessment. If there has been wrong behavior on your part, ask forgiveness. If you feel you are right and the offending party is in denial, take two or three with you who can confirm your assessment. Finally, proclaim today's decrees over your life to insure you are operating from a humble, contrite spirit with no anger for the other person.

_____

_____

_____

_____

_____

_____

_____

_____

_____

_____

_____

_____

_____

SPEAK BLESSING OVER CLIENTS AND CUSTOMERS

Don't allow self-promotion to hide in your hearts,
but in authentic humility put others first
and view others as more important than yourselves.

PHILIPPIANS 2:3 TPT

I moved to Atlanta in 1980. I visited the headquarters of Chick-fil-A on several occasions during my time there, met the founder Truett Cathy, and got to know his son Dan who wrote the foreword to my book *Upside of Adversity*. I have lead the devotional time among their staff at their corporate offices on two occasions. I've watched God bless Chick- fil-A over the last thirty-five years, and I've seen them grow into the top fast-food chicken restaurant in the nation, even surpassing Kentucky Fried Chicken in the last few years.

When my wife and I are looking for a quick meal, it's always going to be Chick-fil-A. I often tell my wife that they have figured out how to get people through their drive thru better than any other fast food chain in America, and their representatives are always courteous and genuinely friendly. When Chick-fil-A employees say to you, "My pleasure," you get the feeling they really mean it.

No doubt, the DNA of service is their kingdom business philosophy. Chick-fil-A's founder, S. Truett Cathy, described that philosophy when he said, "We should be about more than just selling chicken. We should be a part of our customers' lives and the communities in which we serve." The company boasts those words on its website, and customers return time and time again to experience that personal service.

The secular industry has recognized this about Chick-fil-A as well. A recent report ranked the chain as offering the best fast-food customer service in America, beating out In-N-Out Burger and Whataburger, which placed second and third, respectively. After surveying 20,000 fast food customers across the U.S., *Newsweek* and Statista compiled the information into America's Best Customer Service 2020 report. The survey asked customers to rate several brands based on specific elements of service, such as communication, customer focus, professional competence, accessibility, and meeting customer expectations.

Chick-fil-A's score far exceed those of its competitors. This is no surprise since customer service is a fundamental part of the company's brand. What is a surprise to many in the secular business world is that Chick-fil-A does more business than its competitors despite being open only six days a week and closed on Sundays. But on those six days, customers can get delicious chicken, biscuits, waffle fries, and sandwiches served with a sincere smile and genuine respect.[12]

What does it look like in your workplace to model kingdom customer service?

DECREES

I DECREE THAT:

1. I will treat others as more important than myself.
2. I will use my gifts to serve others as a good steward of God's varied grace.
3. I will serve others instead of desiring for them to serve me.
4. I will give because I know it will be given to me in return; good measure, pressed down, shaken together, running over, will be poured into my lap. For with the measure I give, it will be measured back to me.
5. I must be the servant of all if I expect to be first.
6. I understand that when I sow good seed into another person's life, I will reap a harvest.
7. I will be patient and polite with customers and clients that may be upset.
8. I will exceed customer expectations and be a problem solver for my customers.
9. I will have favor with my clients and customers.
10. I will honor God in the way I serve my customers.

Decrees based on the following Scriptures: Ephesians 6:7–8; 1 Peter 4:10; Matthew 20:28; Mark 10:44; Luke 6:38; Mark 9:35; Galatians 6:7

ACTIVATION

The workplace is a great place to model kingdom attributes of servanthood. When you model servant leadership, you stand out among the crowd. Today ask yourself how you can be a better servant in your workplace. What can you do to make yourself or your company stand out among the crowd? What will distinguish you from your competition? Ask God to show you this today and begin an intentional process of implementation.

_____

_____

_____

_____

_____

_____

_____

_____

_____

_____

_____

_____

_____

Day Nineteen

Speak Favor
in Your Community

Seek the peace of the city where I have caused you
to be carried away captive, and pray to the LORD for it;
for in its peace you will have peace.

Jeremiah 29:7 NKJV

If you had met Tim Ulrich in 2007, you probably wouldn't have seen him as they kind of person who takes chances. Comfortable doing youth ministry work at his suburban church, Ulrich led a quiet life in a small California town. To make a living, he used his business degree to buy houses and commercial properties that he renovated and sold for a nice profit. Little did he know that God had bigger plans for him.

With his training and experience in business, Tim assumed he was where he was supposed to be, doing what the Lord expected of him. Besides, he was making good money and getting better at striking deals on properties he knew he could improve. However, one providential business deal turned his life in a new and unexpected direction.

A real estate friend of Tim's told him that there was money to be made in Oklahoma, so Tim and his wife traveled there to make some deals. During their trip, he got a lead on a vacant apartment building. The property owner described the building's location as "thriving" and assured Tim that the property offered great promise to someone with the right flipping skills. Without examining the building himself, Tim accepted the offer and purchased the property.

The truth that Tim would soon discover was that the building was the scene of ongoing criminal activity. Some of the most destitute and desperate people in Oklahoma City stayed in the abandoned building, and those who take advantage of the despair of others made this property their base of operation. Drug lords, prostitutes, and gang members carried on their evil acts, and residents and business owners in the neighborhood hoped that one day someone would level the building to the ground.

When Tim realized that he had been conned and that he now owned a useless and dangerous property, he had no idea where to turn. He was losing $5,000 to $10,000 a month on the property, and he felt his comfortable life slipping away. His only hope was to return to Oklahoma and try to sell the worthless property, knowing he would likely take an even greater loss if he was fortunate enough to find a buyer.

Before heading back to Oklahoma City, he begged God through tears to show him what to do. *I'll do whatever you want, however you want, whenever you want. I'm surrendered. Whatever that means.* And the Lord told Tim to do a remarkable thing. Tim felt God instructing him to give $500 to someone. Even though he had already lost a tremendous amount of money on the deceptive real estate deal, Tim obeyed and sent $500 to a woman he knew was in need. The same day, he received $400 from the same woman.

Confused, Tim decided to open his heart to the lessons on obedience the Lord was trying to teach him. He moved his wife and children from their southern California home to the dilapidated apartment building in Oklahoma City. He decided to become a neighbor to those downtrodden people existing without hope in his building.

Miracles began to happen. Little by little, they worked to fix up the building, which they now called The Refuge, and people from local churches began to pitch in to help. Tim met two men, named Homicide and Tango, generals in the neighborhood gangs. He ministered to them regularly, and the men prayed together. Soon Homicide and Tango asked how they could repent in each of the rooms of the building where they had committed sins.

Local ministries heard what was happening, and they came to see how they could help Tim and his family. They threw a block party for the homeless, attracting the attention of even more churches and ministries, who were grateful for the transformation occurring in their neighborhood.

The Refuge continues to grow, modeling Christ's love to people the rest of the world seemed to have forgotten. With the transformation of the building, the neighborhood was renewed. Ministers left the safety of their churches and came to where the need was greatest. Tim's bold commitment to his new community sparked others to join him in being salt and light to a sad and dark population. In addition to redeeming a rundown building, God has worked through Tim to redeem countless lives.[13]

Problem solving and working together as the body of Christ is a key ingredient to community transformation. How will you be an instrument of transformation to your community?

DECREES

I DECREE THAT:

1. I will let my light shine before men so they may see my good works in my community.
2. I will look for problems in my community that businesses and churches can work together to solve.
3. I will carry other's burdens and fulfill God's purpose in my community.
4. I will be a friend at all times to those in my community and love my neighbor as myself.
5. I will live humbly, living with and identifying with those in low position.
6. I consider as my friends those less fortunate than me in my community.
7. I will lay down my life for my friends in my community.
8. I will spur others to good deeds in my community.
9. There will be no division in the body; its parts will have equal concern for each other. So, too, shall it be in my community.
10. I will love my community deeply because love covers a multitude of sins.

Decrees based on the following Scriptures: Matthew 5:16; John 4:39; 1 Corinthians 1:10; Galatians 6:2; Proverbs 17:17; Romans 12:16; John 15:12; Hebrews 10:24; 1 Corinthians 12:25–27; 1 Peter 4:8–11; Leviticus 19:15–18; Acts 2:44–47

ACTIVATION

Every community has its rough places. Crime, drugs, prostitution, etc. But how do we as the body of Christ have an impact in those areas that the devil controls? We become salt and light in those areas. We become intentional about being the solution to bring light into the darkness. Over the years I have observed there is a "trinity" of community transformation made up of intercessors, business leaders, and churches in a community. When they work together to solve a problem, they have influence in that community. That is how the gospel penetrates a community.

Today ask God to show you the areas in your community that need the salt and light of Christ's redeeming love. If you are a workplace leader, could you bring together those who might be a solution? Write down areas in your community that need God's touch, and pray for God to raise up those who can be the solution. If you are a business owner, could you do something?

_____

_____

_____

_____

_____

_____

_____

_____

_____

_____

SPEAK TO REBELLION

They gathered together against Moses and Aaron,
and said to them, "You take too much upon yourselves,
for all the congregation is holy, every one of them,
and the Lord is among them. Why then do you exalt
yourselves above the assembly of the Lord?"

NUMBERS 16:3 NKJV

One of the great movies of our time is *Braveheart*. It is the story of William Wallace from Scotland. The tyrannical King Edward "Longshanks" was leading England. He murdered Wallace's wife, which ignited in Wallace a revolt against England and the king. Many of the Scottish commoners had also suffered from the heavy hand of the English, and that led them to join Wallace in the revolt. The nobles represented the upper-class landowners. Their leader was Robert the Bruce, the next in line to become King of Scotland. Wallace appealed to Robert the Bruce to join him in the rebellion, but he could not get the landowners to join him in his quest. In fact, Bruce ended up betraying Wallace by setting him up for capture by the king in return for protecting the lands of the nobles. In 1314, Robert, now Scotland's king, repents of his actions. He comes to meet the king to proclaim allegiance to England. In a stunning change of heart, he begins to ride toward the English but stops and invokes Wallace's memory, imploring his men to fight with him as they did with Wallace. Robert then leads his army into battle against the stunned English, winning the Scots their freedom.

There are situations that call for rebellion against ungodly and tyrannical rulership. There are other times when rebellion is made against God's assigned leader, such as in the case of Moses. Korah raised up the people against God's leader and paid the price for it.

Gossip in a workplace is often the seed that begins to foster discontentment and rebellion within a company and its employees. Below is the litmus test cited in *Inc*. magazine for determining whether your conversation is gossip and the consequences it can lead to:

> If your chatter includes rejoicing when others suffer misfortune, that is gossip. If your conversations stir up negative emotions or perpetuate an atmosphere of negativity, that is gossip. If your words are hurtful to someone, are damaging to another either personally or professionally, or are words you would not say to the person's face, that is gossip. If your contribution to a conversation about a fellow employee is rumor, such as unsubstantiated hearsay that someone is getting promoted or demoted, that is gossip. Gossip in the workplace can carry many negative consequences, including the following: You may see your colleagues and employees losing trust, and morale in the workplace may begin to decline. People who feed on the drama will be less productive the more emotionally involved they become. You may notice clusters of discontented employees wasting time chattering at each other's cubicles or stopping each other to catch up on the latest when they should be working. The workplace environment may be tense and anxious as employees hear rumors

and wonder what they should and should not believe. Factions may form as people choose sides. You may have to deal with high turn-over and the loss of valuable employees who prefer not to work in a toxic environment.[14]

Today we decree words to foster trust, mutual respect, and godly leadership in our workplace.

DECREES

I DECREE THAT:

1. No unwholesome word shall proceed from my mouth but only what is helpful in building up others.
2. I will not spread false reports about people or our workplace.
3. I refuse to slander or judge another person. I will honor our leadership.
4. I will always go to a person privately to confirm a matter for its truthfulness.
5. I will be prudent by holding my tongue when I hear something that is negative about a person or our workplace.
6. I will be a person who is trustworthy to keep a matter in confidence.
7. I will encourage others who begin to gossip to go to the person involved to discuss the matter.
8. I will stand against unrighteousness and lawlessness should God call me to.
9. I will obey the government authorities as long as they do not violate God's laws.
10. I will love my neighbor as myself.

Decrees based on the following Scriptures: Ephesians 4:29;
Exodus 3:21; James 1:26; James 4:11; Proverbs 10:19; Proverbs 11:19;
Proverbs 16:28; Proverbs 18:21; Acts 5:29; Romans 13:1–2; Titus 3:1;
Leviticus 19:18

ACTIVATION

Living a godly life in Christ in a pressure packed world can challenge even the best Christian. Factions in workplaces, governments, and even churches can quickly arise through gossip and discontent. Today choose to be a person who honors those in authority over you and avoid gossip in your relationships and workplace. Repent of any gossip in which you may have participated and recommit your life to honoring those over you and those you work with.

_____

_____

_____

_____

_____

_____

_____

_____

_____

_____

_____

_____

_____

_____

SPEAK A NEW IDENTITY

*If anyone is enfolded into Christ, he has become an entirely
new creation. All that is related to the old order has vanished.
Behold, everything is fresh and new.*

2 CORINTHIANS 5:17 TPT

The nightmare began when Pamela was five years old.
Her father asked her to come upstairs and lie down on the bed
with him for a few minutes. She was told if she did, she would
get that puppy she so desperately wanted. What took place next
was something no five-year-old should ever have to experience.
The sexual abuse would continue throughout her young life. It
would happen through another "friend of the family" when she
got older. But this time it was more serious. The abuse was hard-
core and under the threat of death if she told anyone. Pamela was
introduced to drugs at a very early age. Drugs seemed to deaden
the pain of the abuse. This led her into a life of drugs, alcohol, and
even prostitution with wealthy men.

Her grandmother played a positive influence in Pamela's life.
She remembered a time when she was five years old and was visiting
at her grandmother's country farmhouse for Sunday dinner. An old
preacher laid his hand on her head and said, "This one is special.
God is going to use this one." She never forgot those words.

Her life became unbearable at times. She attempted suicide
but failed. Pamela came to Christ at twenty-six, but the demons
inside her kept her from getting free. She was in and out of jail for

drug possession. One night a former drug client set Pamela up. She was arrested and went to prison to serve an 18-month sentence. Strangely, that prison sentence became Pamela's ticket to true freedom. She was finally away from her abuser. She was away from the drugs. She was allowed to start a new life, and she did.

Pamela poured herself into the passages of the Bible, memorizing Scripture for two and a half hours a day. After hearing Pamela praise God audibly in her cell, the other women would ask her to pray for them. She had real joy that spread to other inmates, and she began helping women get free from their demons. She saw many women get delivered of demons and get free for the first time in their lives. Pamela started a group inside the prison called Daughters of Zion, Using Your Time Wisely.

The time came for Pamela to leave, and the women said, "Don't forget us Pamela! Most people forget us!"

"I won't forget you," said Pamela. And she didn't.

She started a ministry called LifeChangers Legacy. She began a one-on-one mentoring program for those in prison. Many in prison are being touched and given new identities through the work Pamela is doing.

I first met Pamela at a movie premiere called *Captive*. Strangely, the movie was about a female drug addict who found freedom. I had been single for seven years. She had been single for fifteen years. We were married a year later.

Today Pamela Hillman's ministry is helping men and women in prison across the nation and the world. Visit LifeChangersLegacy.org to hear her story.

DECREES

I DECREE THAT:

1. I am a new creation in Christ; old things have passed away.
2. I am more than a conqueror in Christ.
3. I am the righteousness of God because Jesus paid my debt.
4. I am no longer a slave but a child and an heir through Christ.
5. I am blessed with every spiritual blessing in the heavenly places.
6. I can do all things through Christ who strengthens me.
7. I am victorious in everything I put my hand to.
8. I am blameless because of Christ's death on the cross.
9. I am made complete in Christ.
10. I am the light of the world, a city on a hill.

Decrees based on the following Scriptures: Galatians 2:20;
2 Corinthians 5:17; Romans 8:37; 2 Corinthians 5:21;
Galatians 4:6–7; Ephesians 1:3; Philippians 4:13;
1 Corinthians 15:57; Colossians 1:22; Colossians 2:10;
Matthew 5:14

ACTIVATION

Someone once said that whenever you allow another person to define who you are, you have made that person an idol in your life. If anyone ever said you were no good, you would not amount to anything, or you will never be successful, you know the power of those words. Those words can define you if you let them. However, what we must do is believe what God says about us as a follower of Jesus. We are new creations in Christ with an entirely new identity. Today decree your identity in Christ. Renounce any identity that does not align with what God says about you because of what Jesus did for you on the cross. Decree these statements aloud to God and to your spouse.

_____

_____

_____

_____

_____

_____

_____

_____

_____

_____

_____

_____

SPEAK COURAGE IN TIMES OF UNCERTAINTY

Have I not commanded you? Be strong and courageous.
Do not be afraid; do not be discouraged,
for the Lord your God will be with you wherever you go.

JOSHUA 1:9 NKJV

Victor Yushchenko's 2004 bid for the presidency of Ukraine was tumultuous. He stood for democracy, and he opposed the ruling party, which made him many enemies. In the heat of the election period, Yushchenko fell mysteriously ill. Doctors diagnosed him with dioxin poisoning, an ingredient used in Agent Orange, and it was clear that his political enemies had a hand in it. The assassination attempt left the man barely recognizable with disfiguring scars all over his face.

Nevertheless, he persisted in his campaign to bring democracy to his country. When election day arrived, Yushchenko enjoyed a comfortable lead in the polls. However, the television station, run by the ruling party, announced that Victor Yushchenko had been soundly beaten by the sitting president.

While the nation watched the news broadcast, the deaf community was focused on the lower right-hand corner of the screen where Natalia Dmitruk relayed the election results in Sign Language. Infuriated by the lies she was assigned to translate, she made a bold decision. Instead of interpreting what the broadcaster was saying, she signed, "I'm addressing all the deaf citizens of Ukraine. They are lying, and I'm ashamed to translate those lies. Yushchenko is our president."

Those in the deaf community sprang into action. They contacted their friends and family and told them about the message Natalia had sent them during the news broadcast. Soon Natalia's courageous and defiant act inspired other journalists to report the truth about the election results. To symbolize their rejection of the corrupt election and the poisoning of their candidate by Agent Orange, millions of people in Ukraine wore orange as they took to the streets to demand a new election. Their protests forced the government to concede to a new election in which the people of Ukraine elected Victor Yushchenko their new president.[15]

People who play it safe are not the subject of books and movies. Books and movies are about people who make a difference in the world at great risk to their own lives. Sometimes courage is required to stand in the face of unrighteousness and lies, as in the case of Natalia and her government. She had only a few moments to decide what she would do. She knew what was being said was a lie. Would she simply be a pawn of the unrighteous government, or would she risk her life to stand for truth? Her courageous stand changed the destiny of a nation.

What stand has God called you to make? What will be written about your life?

DECREES

I DECREE THAT:

1. I will be a strong and courageous leader.
2. God will always be with me to strengthen me and help me.
3. As I wait for the Lord, God will make me strong.
4. As I trust in the Lord and avoid leaning on my own understanding, God will make my path straight.
5. Even though I walk through the darkest valley, I will fear no evil, for God is with me; his rod and his staff, they comfort me.
6. Goodness and love will follow me all the days of my life, and I will dwell in the house of the Lord forever.
7. I choose to trust in the Lord in the face of bad news.
8. God is able to do immeasurably more than I ask or imagine, according to his power that is at work within me.
9. I will not fear, for God is always with me, to help me and uphold me with his right hand.
10. The Lord is on my side; I will not fear. What can man do unto me?

Decrees based on the following Scriptures: Joshua 1:9; Psalm 27:14; Proverbs 3:5–6; Psalm 23:2–4; Psalm 112:7; Ephesians 3:20; Isaiah 41:10; Psalm 118:6

ACTIVATION

Life has a way of bringing events into our life that can tempt us to fear. It could be a layoff, news of cancer, a false accusation, standing against ungodly leadership, a marriage crisis, a lost deal—the opportunities to fear life situations are limitless. However, we can choose not to fear. We can choose to place our lives in the hands of our master. We can let him lead us and be our strength in these times. Are you faced with a situation that needs courage and faith? Decree these statements out loud and let these words build faith in you, no matter the circumstance. Tell God you trust him to protect you and guide you through this time.

_____

_____

_____

_____

_____

_____

_____

_____

_____

_____

_____

_____

_____

SPEAK ENCOURAGEMENT

The people that do know their God shall be strong,
and do exploits.
DANIEL 11:32 KJV

Earlier I told you about the rebellion of William Wallace of Scotland against King Edward of England. One of the great movie scenes of all time was in the movie *Braveheart*. The commoners of Scotland were about to go to battle against the massive army of King Edward Longshanks at Stirling. They were severely outnumbered and out armed. William Wallace had been winning small battles against the troops of England. Many of the commoners had not seen Wallace yet; they had only heard of his heroic exploits. He was a larger-than-life figure based on the tales others told about his feats in conquering England's armies.

The nobles brought this small band of ordinary citizens together to fight the English. However, the commoners felt they were simply fighting to gain more land for the nobles rather than achieving freedom for their nation of Scotland. Then Wallace showed up in battle paint with his band of renegades and made this amazing speech:

> Sons of Scotland, I am William Wallace... I am
> William Wallace! And I see a whole army of
> my countrymen here in defiance of tyranny.

You have come to fight as free men, and free men you are. What would you do without freedom? Will you fight?… Aye, fight and you may die. Run and you'll live, at least a while. And dying in your beds many years from now, would you be willing to trade all the days from this day to that for one chance, just one chance to come back here and tell our enemies that they may take our lives, but they'll never take…our freedom! *Alba gu brath!*[16]

Wallace led his band of commoners to victory that day because they were fighting for a cause greater than themselves. But it took a leader to instill courage and faith to engage them into battle.

As a leader, you are called to inspire others to do great things. In the workplace, many situations arise to dampen the spirits of the employees. Whether you are the CEO, the manager, or a worker, you play a vital role in being a catalyst to inspire your team to overcome whatever obstacles might be in your midst.

DECREES

I DECREE THAT:

1. I will be one who sharpens my fellow teammate because iron sharpens iron.
2. I will use my gifts and talents to inspire great things from my team.
3. I will be like-minded with my fellow workers to work as a team.
4. I will provoke my team to love and good deeds.
5. There will be no divisions among us, but we will be perfectly joined in the same mind and in the same judgment.
6. My team is not one member but many, working together for a greater cause.
7. We will let nothing be done through strife or vainglory, but in lowliness of mind, we will esteem others as better than ourselves.
8. I will look not only to my own interests but also to the interests of others.
9. I will discourage scoffers so strife will go out and quarreling and abuse will cease.
10. I will preach the Word! I'll be ready in season and out of season. I will convince, rebuke, exhort, with all longsuffering and teaching.

*Decrees based on the following Scriptures: Proverbs 27:17;
1 Peter 4:10; Romans 15:5; Hebrews 10:24; 1 Corinthians 1:10;
1 Corinthians 12:4; Philippians 2:3; 1 Timothy 4:2*

ACTIVATION

We all need encouragement. We need to be inspired to go the distance, to achieve something greater. As a leader, your call from God is to inspire others to fulfill their greatest capacity. Inspiring one can inspire others. Like Wallace, look for opportunities to inspire your coworkers today. Affirm the positive qualities that you see in them. Today you will make someone's day!

_____

_____

_____

_____

_____

_____

_____

_____

_____

_____

_____

_____

_____

_____

SPEAK ENDURANCE

*Even in the midst of all these things, we triumph over them
all, for God has made us to be more than conquerors, and his
demonstrated love is our glorious victory over everything!*

ROMANS 8:37 TPT

The year 1994 was my year from hell … or was it from heaven?
In the first three months, events led to the loss of 80 percent of my
business, my wife leaving me, and a complete loss of my wealth.
During that time, my vice president left and stole my second-
largest account in my ad agency. This ushered me into a seven-year
season of struggle. Two years into my season, a man said, "Os, you
have a 'Joseph Calling' on your life. It is a marketplace call. God is
calling you into this."

I had no clue what he was talking about. All I knew was that
if anyone knew about these thing, this man would know. Gunnar
Olson was the founder of the International Christian Chamber of
Commerce. He had a better understanding of a marketplace call
than anyone else in the world. That day he became my spiritual
father in the marketplace. Years later, I could see that every word
he said would come true. Seven years later, God restored my
finances and birthed an international workplace ministry that
would allow me to write twenty books and train leaders in twenty-
eight countries. He turned my Valley of Achor (trouble) into a
door of hope.

Joseph must have felt the same way. He was thrust into a pit only to be sold to a caravan of foreign slave traders. He would end up being a slave of the Egyptian Potiphar's house. We all know this story. He eventually spends time in prison for a crime he did not commit and interprets a dream for Pharaoh that gets him out of prison. He later understands the truth about his life when he makes this amazing statement to his brothers who caused his hardship: "God sent me ahead of you to preserve you…. You meant to harm me, but God intended it for a good purpose" (Genesis 45:7, 50:20 NET).

Seeing adversity through the lens of eternity is key to having the grace to walk through it successfully. When God allows you to go through adversity, it will always result in an upgrade with God if you press into him with all your heart. The good news is that only Jesus made plan A; God turns our B plans and C plans into his A plans. He is a redemptive God who turns all things into good if we will trust him. His nature is always redemptive.

God often uses what happens to us in the workplace as a catalyst to mature us in him. So many things can go wrong in your work life calling that require you to make major adjustments in your life. Recessions, changing market conditions, product failure, and employee revolts are just a few things that can go wrong in a business.

Today, we are going to look at decrees that proclaim God's goodness and trust in God's omnipotence to use even the most difficult things in our life for his purposes.

DECREES

I DECREE THAT:

1. God is continually weaving together every detail of my life to fit into his perfect plan of bringing good into my life.
2. No weapon formed against me shall prosper.
3. No matter how bad my circumstances are, I will praise God, for he holds my hand and my future in his hand.
4. I will be strong and courageous because God is with me no matter what I encounter.
5. I will keep my peace because my mind will stay upon God.
6. God will uphold me with his right hand.
7. I will walk in peace that God gives me; it is not the world's peace but God's peace.
8. I will trust in the Lord with all my heart; I will not lean on my own understanding.
9. I am the righteousness of Christ. When I cry out, the Lord hears me. He is close to the brokenhearted and those crushed in spirit.
10. His grace is sufficient for me because I know that his power is made perfect in weakness.

Decrees based on the following Scriptures: Romans 8:28; Isaiah 54:17; Habakkuk 3:18; Deuteronomy 31:6; Isaiah 26:3; Isaiah 41:10; John 14:26; Proverbs 3:5–6; Psalm 34:17–18; 2 Corinthians 12:9

ACTIVATION

God often ushers us into the larger story of our life through a crisis. David, Joseph, Paul, and many others began their journey with God with a crisis. If you find yourself in a crisis, do not fear. Put your faith in the living God who knows what you are going through. Make these decrees daily. Do not let the enemy impugn the nature of God to make you think he does not care. Our temptation is to believe a lie—that God does not care about you and is not working on your behalf. Sometimes it requires time to see your situation turn for the better. Make a commitment today to place your faith in God, who cares for you. He demonstrated this on the cross by dying for you. That is where the love question was answered once and for all.

_____

_____

_____

_____

_____

_____

_____

_____

_____

_____

_____

DAY TWENTY-FIVE

SPEAK YOUR VISION

*The Lord answered me and said: "Write the vision and
make it plain on tablets, that he may run who reads it.
For the vision is yet for an appointed time; but at the end it
will speak, and it will not lie. Though it tarries, wait for it;
because it will surely come, it will not tarry."*

HABAKKUK 2:2–3 NKJV

"If you aim at nothing, you will hit it every time," said sales trainer Zig Ziglar. God gave us a vision for our lives. In Jeremiah, he says, "'For I know the plans I have for you,' declares the Lord, 'plans to prosper you and not to harm you, plans to give you a hope and a future.'" Jeremiah was speaking to the nation of Israel, but this statement is for every person who follows God. He also tells us in John 10:10 that Jesus came to give us life and life abundantly. Satan wants to destroy the vision God has for your life. He says that his mission is to steal, kill, and destroy your life (John 10:10). Isn't that interesting? Two vision statements in one sentence. God's vision is life abundantly, and Satan's is death.

Proverbs tells us that if there is not revelation of a vision, the people are scattered in their ways. Getting revelation means you are operating in wisdom according to Proverbs 29:18 (TPT): "When there is no clear prophetic vision, people quickly wander astray. But when you follow the revelation of the word, heaven's bliss fills your soul." People who write down their visions are much more likely to fulfill their visions than those who do not write them down.

Have you ever seen an Olympic gymnast in the moments just before he or she participates in the vault event? You can watch the athlete's face as they perform the jump over and over in their mind, perfecting each move while standing perfectly still. This is visualization, and many secular researchers have learned that the process of visualization can be almost as effective as performing the act with your body.

The mind and body do not work separately from each other. Our brain's neurons interpret the mental images we conjure in the same way they interpret reality. You can combine visualization with faith, too, and this combination can be a potent and powerful tool. For example, you can imagine yourself in a situation where you want to be, your dream job, a successful career, a profitable company, a thriving ministry. The more you visualize this, the more you strengthen your faith that you can accomplish your goal. Your brain will respond to this.

Professional golfers take time to imagine their shots before they swing at the ball. Baseball pitchers envision their pitches going across the plate. Long before achieving his status as the heavyweight champion of the world, Muhammad Ali visualized himself as the greatest boxer who ever lived. You need to see yourself as a success in your mind.[17]

There is something significant about handwriting our visions too. This allows us to have a clear record of what we envision. It gives us something tangible to refer to as we pray and decree over our vision. It allows us to slow down our brains and absorb what we are writing. Perhaps that is why the prophet said, "Write down the vision and make it plain." Today, consider journaling daily about what you want to see happen in your life.

DECREES

I DECREE THAT:

1. I will write down my vision and believe it will be fulfilled.
2. I will see myself fulfilling my vision.
3. I will ask God to give me visions in the night of his purposes for my life.
4. I commit whatever I do to the Lord so that it might be established.
5. I will sit down and estimate the cost to see if I have enough money and resources to complete my plan. I will trust God for what I need.
6. God will give me the desires of my heart and make my plans succeed.
7. I may plan my course, but it is the Lord who establishes my steps.
8. I affirm that there is a time for everything and a season for every activity under the heavens.
9. I will trust in the Lord to fulfill my plans because my confidence is in him.
10. I will not be anxious about anything, but in every situation, by prayer and petition, with thanksgiving, I will present my requests to God. And the peace of God, which transcends all understanding, will guard my heart and mind in Christ Jesus.

Decrees based on the following Scriptures: Jeremiah 29:11; John 10:10; Numbers 12:6; Proverbs 29:18; Proverbs 16:3; Luke 14:28; Psalm 20:4; Ecclesiastes 3:1; Jeremiah 17:7; Philippians 4:6–7

ACTIVATION

Has God put a dream in your heart? Write that dream down. Pray over it. Plan what it will take to see that vision become a reality. Get counsel from others. Believe in your vision. Write down the vision below and put it where you can see it daily. Ask God to show you what you need to know about that vision. Then step toward that dream with actions needed to see it become a reality.

_____

_____

_____

_____

_____

_____

_____

_____

_____

_____

_____

_____

_____

_____

_____

_____

_____

SPEAK FREEDOM
AND BOUNDARIES

*The Lord God took the man and put him in the garden of
Eden to tend and keep it. And the Lord God commanded the
man, saying, "Of every tree of the garden you may freely
eat; but of the tree of the knowledge of good and evil you shall
not eat, for in the day that you eat of it you shall surely die."*

GENESIS 2:15–17 NKJV

God made man to operate with freedoms and boundaries in his life. Freedoms allowed man to exercise dominion over the area God entrusted to him. Boundaries protected man from getting into areas that would be harmful to him.

This is what God established soon after his creation of man. Adam and Eve made a big mistake when they crossed into areas where God had set a boundary. In fact, it changed the course of human history because sin came into the world as a result of violating that boundary.

Living a life of integrity means we live within the spiritual boundaries God set for us described in the Bible. In the workplace, we all need freedoms and boundaries. We need to be entrusted with the authority to make decisions as they relate to our area of expertise and job description. If we are not given freedom to have authority within our realm of responsibility, we will feel controlled and limited in our ability to succeed. Managers that micro-manage do their company and their employees a disservice and fail to foster an environment where their people can grow. Your staff needs to be able to make mistakes and learn from them.

Boundaries must be honored within a company. If we go beyond a boundary set up by our company, then we might suffer from a mistake that could be costly to the organization. Make sure you know your freedoms and your boundaries. Sometimes this is not clearly spelled out and leaves employees to guess where those freedoms and boundaries exist.

God set up places in the garden that allowed Adam and Eve to prosper in all they put their hand to. He also told them there were areas that would be harmful to them and that they needed to avoid those areas. God's Word also gives us freedoms and boundaries. It tells us things we should avoid and things we should embrace to have a successful life.

Mary Kay Ash, founder of Mary Kay Cosmetics, once said, "Many women have made the mistake of changing their beliefs to accommodate their work. It must be the other way around. No circumstance is so unusual that it demands a double standard or separates us from our faith. No matter how fast the world changes, exemplary values must remain constant."[18]

Today, learn your freedoms and boundaries in work and life.

DECREES

I DECREE THAT:

1. I will live within the boundaries God has set for me. I will live a life of integrity.
2. God has set the time in which I would live on earth and the boundaries within which I will live and work.
3. I will set healthy boundaries to the number of hours I will work to maintain healthy margins in my life.
4. I will set times of prayer and solitude to ensure a balanced life.
5. I will remain focused on the assignment I have been given and not be drawn into tasks that take me away from my calling.
6. I will choose my words carefully in responding to those who seek to cause division in my workplace.
7. I will remain focused on my unique assignment and will avoid letting others manipulate me for their own agenda.
8. I will oversee my team to make sure we are operating in the boundaries of our assignments.
9. I acknowledge and embrace God's boundaries for my protection and well-being.
10. I will identify my priorities and set my schedule accordingly in order to achieve my goals.

Decrees based on the following Scriptures: Psalm 16:6; Acts 17:26; Matthew 12:46–50; Matthew 21:23–27, 22:15–22; Matthew 16:23; Matthew 21:12–17; John 2:12–16; Matthew 6:6; Luke 16:13; Psalm 51

ACTIVATION

Setting healthy freedoms and boundaries is required if you want to maintain a balanced and fruitful life. Jesus modeled this so well. He set times to pray. He refused to let others draw him into battles he was not called to. He knew where he was to travel. He knew how much personal time he needed to spend with his disciples. He knew what he was called to and what he wasn't called to. Today spend some time evaluating areas of your life. Are you outside some boundaries in the way you spend your time? Write down any situations you need to correct. Are there any areas where you are not exercising your freedoms? Write those down. Pray for God's perfect balance in your life.

_____

_____

_____

_____

_____

_____

_____

_____

_____

_____

_____

_____

SPEAK CULTURAL IMPACT

Don't hide your light! Let it shine brightly before others,
so that the commendable things you do will shine as light
upon them, and then they will give their praise to your
Father in heaven.

MATTHEW 5:16 TPT

We're living in a day in which we are seeing many of the spiritual values and foundations that have made our nation great disintegrate right before our eyes. Espousing Christian values is being called bigotry. Having an absolute biblical worldview is being narrow minded. Citing what the Bible says about homosexuality is preaching intolerance. Free speech is hate speech unless it agrees with the left's worldview. The enemy of our souls is seeking to change the language in the culture. Isaiah foretold this when he said, "Woe to those who call evil good, and good evil; Who put darkness for light, and light for darkness; Who put bitter for sweet, and sweet for bitter!" (Isaiah 5:20 NKJV).

Jesus talked a great deal about the kingdom of God. He did not come to give just the kingdom of salvation but also the kingdom of God in every area of society. That's why a nation that has a lot of Christians will not change unless they live what the Bible says. When Jesus prayed in the Lord's Prayer that he wanted us to bring heaven on earth just as it is in heaven, that was a commission given by our Lord for all believers.

In *How Now Shall We Live?*, Chuck Colson and Nancy Pearcey summarize our call to be salt and light in our culture:

> God cares not only about redeeming souls but also about restoring his creation. He calls us to be agents not only of his saving grace but also of his common grace. Our job is not only to build up the church but also to build a society to the glory of God. As agents of God's common grace, we are called to help sustain and renew his creation, to uphold the created institutions of family and society, to pursue science and scholarship, to create works of art and beauty, and to heal and help those suffering from the results of the fall.[19]

Imagine if every person in the workplace modeled the Lord's Prayer by bringing heaven into their sphere of influence. We would have a radically different society. Today let us decree that we will renew our hearts to be salt and light in a culture that so desperately needs his love and to bring heaven on earth.

DECREES

I DECREE THAT:

1. I will be salt and light in all that I do for the glory of God. I will proclaim truth to give freedom to all.
2. I will stand for righteousness when the culture is seeking to destroy our Christian values.
3. I will be a voice to give a word in season that needs to be voiced.
4. I will seek to bring heaven on earth in every sphere of society.
5. Jesus will reign so that all his enemies shall be put under his feet.
6. I will join Jesus in building his kingdom on earth so the gates of hell will not prevail against it.
7. I will pray for repentance and revival in our nation, for that is the only real way we will see culture impacted.
8. I will humble myself and seek his face so that he might forgive our nation and heal our land.
9. I will seek to be a problem solver like Jesus, for that is a primary way we have influence in society.
10. I will build bridges with those who have different values than I so that I might win some through my engagement with them.

Decrees based on the following Scriptures: 1 Peter 3:15; Isaiah 5:20; Matthew 6:9–13; 1 Corinthians 15:25; Matthew 16:18; 2 Chronicles 7:14; 1 Corinthians 9:19–23; John 8:32

ACTIVATION

Never before have we seen culture being built upon lies like today. Fake news. Political manipulation. Power grabs. Distortions of facts. We live in a day that requires us to be gentle as doves but wise as serpents. We cannot win the culture war using the same weapons as those who oppose our Christian values. Today commit yourself to being God's representative by being a person of prayer, engagement, truth telling, love, bridge building, and courage. Stand for the truth where others promote unrighteousness. Be salt and light where God takes you. Be his voice. List the areas where you can make the greatest difference in the culture and begin praying about how to engage.

_____

_____

_____

_____

_____

_____

_____

_____

_____

_____

_____

_____

DAY TWENTY-EIGHT

SPEAK PRAISE
IN ALL THINGS

Your tender mercies mean more to me than life itself.
How I love and praise you, God! Daily I will worship you
passionately and with all my heart. My arms will wave to
you like banners of praise. I overflow with praise when I come
before you, for the anointing of your presence satisfies me
like nothing else.

PSALM 63:3–5 TPT

Bestselling author A. J. Jacobs describes himself as a human guinea pig and his life as a series of experiments. As an example of a journalist who immerses himself in the subjects of his research, Jacobs spent an entire year strictly abiding by the moral codes in the Old Testament before writing *The Year of Living Biblically: One Man's Humble Quest to Follow the Bible as Literally as Possible.*

In *The Guinea Pig Diaries: My Life as an Experiment*, a series of essays Jacobs wrote during an all-encompassing quest for self-improvement, the author subjected his family to an authentic Thanksgiving Day as the Pilgrims might have celebrated it in 1621. This included wild turkey stew, lobster, and eel, eaten without utensils. They played games, told riddles, and held races as the Pilgrims likely did. Jacobs marveled that such a time of celebration and gratitude came so soon after the tragic death of forty-eight of the 102 original Pilgrims due to scurvy and exposure.

Nevertheless, they celebrated, rejoiced, and gave thanks. Jacobs concluded that, "If they could appreciate life amid such chaos, pain, and uncertainty, I could give thanks for all the good things in my relatively cushy life."[20]

No matter how bad you think things might be in your life, others' situations can always make your ordeal seem small in comparison. Just this week I read of a family of six driving to enjoy a family event when another driver crossed the median and hit their car. Five members of the family perished, and only the mother survived. Life can seem cruel at times. The Bible says it rains on the just and the unjust.

The key to overcoming difficult places in our lives is finding something for which we can praise God. We don't praise God for the negative events; we praise God for his ability to sustain us and to make all things work together for good in the midst of the pain. We praise him for being God and his attributes of love, righteousness, and justice.

The prophet Habakkuk saw his resources crumbling when he lamented:

> Though the fig tree may not blossom,
> nor fruit be on the vines;
> Though the labor of the olive may fail,
> and the fields yield no food;
> Though the flock may be cut off from the
> fold, and there be no herd in the stalls—
> Yet I will rejoice in the Lord,
> I will joy in the God of my salvation.
> (Habakkuk 3:17–18 NKJV)

The prophet Isaiah realized the only way to overcome depression was to do the opposite—praise God in the midst of his situation. "To console those who mourn in Zion, to give them beauty for ashes, the oil of joy for mourning, the garment of praise for the spirit of heaviness; That they may be called trees of righteousness, the planting of the LORD, that He may be glorified" (Isaiah 61:3 NKJV).

Do you find yourself in a difficult place? Submit your situation to the Lord. Offer a prayer of praise to God for his love and grace in your life. It may not change your circumstance, but it will change how you deal with your situation.

DECREES

I DECREE THAT:

1. I will praise God no matter how difficult my life is right now.
2. I will overcome a spirit of heaviness as I praise God.
3. I will sing praises to the Lord's name because he is worthy of my praise.
4. I praise the Lord for being the everlasting God, the Creator of the ends of the earth.
5. I praise the Lord that he does not faint or grow weary; his understanding is unsearchable.
6. I praise the Lord, for his way is perfect. I praise him that his Word proves true and that he is a shield for all those who take refuge in him.
7. I praise the Lord for his holiness. "Holy, holy, holy is the Lord of hosts; the whole earth is full of His glory!"
8. I praise the Lord, who is like no other, pardoning iniquity and passing over transgression.
9. I praise the Lord for being a God who is merciful and gracious, slow to anger, and abounding in steadfast love and faithfulness, keeping steadfast love for thousands, forgiving iniquity and transgression and sin, but who will by no means clear the guilty.
10. I will praise God, whose might is like no other and whose faithfulness surrounds him. I praise him that righteousness and justice are the foundation of his throne and that steadfast love and faithfulness go before him.

Decrees based on the following Scriptures: Habakkuk 3:17–18; Isaiah 25:1; Psalm 150:6; Acts 16:25; Psalm 42:11; Psalm 103:1; Isaiah 40:28; Psalm 18:30; Isaiah 6:3; Micah 7:18; Exodus 34:6–7; Psalm 89:8,14

ACTIVATION

Today acknowledge that God is Lord over all life and circumstances. Recommit your life to God and entrust all circumstances into his care. Today you become a person of praise. You acknowledge the Lord over all your circumstances. Although you do not understand all the ways of God, you choose to praise him no matter the outcomes. Decree these words of praise out loud.

_____

_____

_____

_____

_____

_____

_____

_____

_____

_____

_____

_____

_____

SPEAK TO YOUR ENEMIES

Love your enemy, bless the one who curses you, do something
wonderful for the one who hates you, and respond to the very
ones who persecute you by praying for them. What reward do
you deserve if you only love the loveable? Don't even the tax
collectors do that?

MATTHEW 5:44,46 TPT

I once had a conflict with a client when I had my own ad agency. This client was my largest account. An issue arose around the job we did. We did our best to correct it and make good on it. Nevertheless, the client used this to fire us and stick us with a $140,000 bill. We filed a lawsuit against the client. He countersued me. A mentor advised me to reconsider the situation. He said if I had any wrong in the process, even if it were 2 percent, I had to own it. That led to me forgiving the lawsuit even before he retracted his lawsuit. The client refused to take any ownership of the issue, and I had the obligation of paying all the costs related to the project. It took me five years to pay all the related debts. I decided to follow what the Scripture said, to forgive and bless my enemies. I called the man and went to dinner with him. Deep down I thought, *Well, maybe he will own his part now that I removed my lawsuit.* But he didn't. I had to let go of the situation and put it in God's hands.

Sometimes doing the right thing is costly. However in the scheme of eternity, we need to view it as a small thing. Jesus' obedience took him to the cross. He washed the feet of his accuser. Blessing our enemies can be an extremely hard thing to do. However, God calls each of us to do just that. He says if we don't forgive those who wrong us, he will not forgive us. However, forgiving is only the first step. The next step is actually blessing our enemy.

To know if you have forgiven someone, ask yourself this: If their name is mentioned, what happens in your spirit? Do feelings of anger arise? Or maybe fear begins to rule your emotions? When you can hear that person's name and not have a negative emotion, you will know you are free and you have truly forgiven.

Let go and let God. Sometimes we must let God be the judge of our enemy's actions against us. I believe our obedience is measured back to us in other ways down the road. God has blessed my life in many other ways since that event.

DECREES

I DECREE THAT:

1. God will put all my enemies beneath my feet.
2. I will walk in wisdom to know how to defeat my enemies.
3. I will put my trust in the Lord to protect me from my enemies.
4. The God in me is greater than he that is in the world.
5. I will bless my enemies so that it will go well with me.
6. I will receive my reward because I feed my enemy and give him water. I will be rewarded.
7. I forgive those who wrongfully accuse me.
8. I will consider trials a joy so that I will become a person of perseverance.
9. The Lord will fight my battles for me.
10. I will not walk in fear but in power, love, and a sound mind.

Decrees based on the following Scriptures: Psalm 35:19–20; Exodus 14:14; 2 Timothy 1:7; James 1:2–3; Proverbs 25:21–22; 1 Peter 4:14; Mark 12:36; Luke 21:15; Psalm 81:14; Psalm 91:11; Matthew 5:44; Psalm 91:14–16

ACTIVATION

If you work, you will eventually have conflict. Accusations, misunderstandings, and dishonesty all have the opportunity to create adversarial relationships. The key is staying on the high ground and not being drawn into a fleshly battle. God's economy is often contrary to the world's in how we deal with conflict and our enemies. God says to love your enemies and even bless them. That does not mean we have to be a doormat. We still need to set boundaries and hold people accountable for their actions. If you find yourself in conflict with someone you consider an enemy, proclaim blessing over his or her life today. Offer forgiveness and pray for that person. This will release you from the burden and put the burden on God to deal with the situation.

_____

_____

_____

_____

_____

_____

_____

_____

_____

_____

_____

DAY THIRTY

SPEAK SUCCESS

*I know what it means to lack, and I know what it means
to experience overwhelming abundance. For I'm trained in
the secret of overcoming all things, whether in fullness or
in hunger. And I find that the strength of Christ's explosive
power infuses me to conquer every difficulty.*

PHILIPPIANS 4:13 TPT

Success cannot be defined merely from a financial statement. We should always measure success by God's measuring stick. He looks at things like character, family, generosity, peace, and devotion to God and the fruit of the Spirit. These define true success in life.

Over the years I have met several successful people. A few years ago, I interviewed David Green, founder of Hobby Lobby. By every measuring stick, you would have to conclude that David has had a successful life.

When David was a boy listening to his father preach in a small, rural church, he may not have expected to grow up to be the CEO of a multi-billion-dollar corporation. However, he may have expected that any endeavor he undertook would glorify God and honor his holy will. In 1970, David secured a $600 bank loan to buy the materials and equipment he needed to make miniature picture frames. That investment grew into Hobby Lobby Stores, Inc., a national arts and crafts chain based in Oklahoma City. Today the

Green family trust controls the proceeds of more than 780 stores in forty-seven states.

Nearing 80, David Green still sees himself as a steward, not the owner, of the company. He believes his success is a result of his trust and obedience. Despite risking millions of dollars annually, Hobby Lobby stores close at 8 p.m., a reasonable time for families, and remain closed on Sundays to honor the Lord's Day. David continues to fulfill a commitment he made to the Lord to support the efforts of Christians around the world. The Greens are generous donors to ministries, schools, and individuals in need, giving away 50 percent of their profits. When faced with a controversial law that would have forced him to compromise his beliefs, David fought all the way to the Supreme Court to protect the rights of closely-held companies from having to provide the morning-after pill in employee health care plans. In 2017, the Green family built the $500 million, state-of-the-art Museum of the Bible in Washington, D.C., which is something everyone should visit.[21]

David did something unusual for a very successful CEO. He legally set limits to the amount of money a family member could receive from the business. Don't get me wrong, they are well taken care of. However, if future generations ever decide to sell the business, the trust will automatically divert 90 percent of the proceeds to a foundation that supports Christian ministries. The Greens have groomed their children and their grandchildren to uphold the Christian values and culture that have made Hobby Lobby so successful. They decide as a family when it is appropriate to make investments.

God doesn't guarantee material success in life. However, when we apply the Word of God to every aspect of life, the net result is often material success and success in our personal lives and relationships. He gives us principles to live by that help us become successful.

Today let us decree God's success over our work and life.

DECREES

I DECREE THAT:

1. I commit to the Lord whatever I do so that he will establish my plans.
2. I will be trustworthy with a little so that I can be trusted with much.
3. I will not conform to the pattern of this world but be transformed by the renewing of my mind through Jesus Christ.
4. God will strengthen me and uphold me by his righteous right hand.
5. I will not be anxious for anything, but through prayer and petition, I will make my request known to God.
6. God gives me the ability to create wealth to confirm his covenant with me.
7. For I know the plans God has for me, plans to prosper me and not to harm me, plans to give me a hope and a future.
8. I will be a shining example of God's light and love through my success and generosity.
9. I will press on toward the goal to win the prize for which God has called me heavenward in Christ Jesus.
10. The Lord makes firm my steps as I delight in him; though I may stumble, I will not fall, for the Lord upholds me with his hand.

Decrees based on the following Scriptures: Psalm 37:4;
Proverbs 16:3; Luke 16:10; Romans 12:2; Isaiah 41:10;
Philippians 4:6; Deuteronomy 8:18; Jeremiah 29:11;
1 Thessalonians 2:12; Philippians 3:13–14; Psalm 37:24

ACTIVATION

Today I want you to see yourself as successful—successful in work, life, and relationships. Declare God's success over your life and start seeing yourself as successful. No matter where you are today, begin to believe and decree success over your life. Agree with God that you will manifest that success in this life. He is for you!

_____

_____

_____

_____

_____

_____

_____

_____

_____

_____

_____

_____

_____

_____

_____

_____

DAY THIRTY-ONE

SPEAK TO DISEASE

Jesus said to her, "Daughter, because you dared to believe,
your faith has healed you. Go with peace in your heart
and be free from your suffering!"
MARK 5:34 TPT

We never appreciate our health until we lose it. Disease can take us away from our work life calling. Whether it's a common cold or cancer, being sick keeps you from enjoying life and fulfilling your purpose on earth. Sickness is never from God. We know this because Jesus prayed that whatever was in heaven would be on earth. There is no sickness in heaven. There is no corruption in heaven. There is no poverty in heaven. So God wants us to bring whatever is in heaven onto the earth through prayer and decree. God decreed in Genesis that the oceans and the animals and the plants would come into being—God decreed literally all creation.

My wife began having severe discomfort in her right foot. It kept her from being able to work. She tried to manage the pain over several months unsuccessfully. We finally had to meet with a surgeon. That led to a painful surgery. The recovery was slow and painful. However, after about five months, she began to feel better. We were planning to go to Israel the following June, so we were pleased that she was getting better.

A few months before we were to leave for Israel, my wife began to have the same kind of pain she had before. We were both devastated at the possibility of another surgery. We went to the surgeon, and he explained what might be going on. It was not a good prognosis. "Should we cancel our trip?" I asked my wife.

My wife has the gift of faith. Her response was, "No, we are going to Israel. I am going to get healed in Israel!"

"Are you sure you want to risk going to Israel with a hurt foot?" I asked.

Her reply was firm. "I'm going to get healed in Israel."

We went to Israel, and on the last three nights of our trip, we participated in a small conference with those who were part of the trip. The leaders of the event were close friends. We asked if they would lay hands on Pamela's foot and pray for healing. When they laid hands on her, she felt heat in her foot. She began walking around without discomfort. The following day she awakened and had no pain. It has now been over a year since our trip to Israel. She has not experienced foot pain since. Truly God is the healer of our bodies!

DECREES

I DECREE THAT:

1. Because Jesus was wounded for our transgressions and bruised for our iniquities and the chastisement for our peace was upon him, I believe that by his stripes I am healed, so I will walk in health.
2. According to my faith I shall be healed.
3. The Lord is with me to overcome all fear and uncertainty.
4. God will restore my health and heal all my wounds.
5. I will overcome a spirit of heaviness with praise.
6. I will see the goodness of the Lord in all things.
7. When I cry unto God, he heals me.
8. Even when I am old, he will sustain me and rescue me.
9. God will shine his light upon my body and my healing will quickly appear.
10. I will never be afraid because God gives me his peace.

Decrees based on the following Scriptures: Isaiah 58:8; Isaiah 61:3; John 14:27; Psalm 30:2; Matthew 9:28–30; Isaiah 41:10; Isaiah 53:5; Jeremiah 30:17

ACTIVATION

Speak to every area of your body today. Decree that each organ will function as God designed it to function. Proclaim that your body was made to heal itself. Invite Jesus into every area of your body that needs healing to live and manifest his life in and through your physical body. Tell whatever symptom is in your body that is not operating correctly to come back into God's alignment. Write out your decree below.

This concludes our thirty-one days, but it is not the end of the book. Start your thirty-one days over again. Do it every day and every month and activate these decrees in your life.

_____

_____

_____

_____

_____

_____

_____

_____

_____

_____

_____

ENDNOTES

1   "Stanley Tam – US Plastic," Giants for God, accessed March 5,
    2020, http://www.giantsforgod.com.

2   "Dr. Masaru Emoto and Water Consciousness," The Wellness
    Enterprise, March 23, 2017, https://thewellnessenterprise.com.

3   "William Wilberforce," BBC, last modified July 5, 2011, https://
    www.bbc.co.uk.

4   Willis, Dave, "7 Marriage Lessons from the Reagans," Time USA,
    LLC, March 9, 2016, https://time.com.

5   Trevor Freeze, "A Story of God's Protection in Joplin," Billy
    Graham Evangelistic Association, June 16, 2011, https://
    billygraham.org.

6   Clayton Berry, "Jesuit Philosopher Recounts Time with Mother
    Teresa," Catholic Education Resource Center, September 4, 2007,
    https://www.catholiceducation.org.

7   Lisa van den Berg, "God Business and Bow Hunting: a Journey of
    Faithfulness," Bethel Church of Redding, October 24, 2016, https://
    heaveninbusiness.com.

8   "9 Things Invented or Discovered by Accident," HowStuffWorks,
    accessed March 4, 2020, https://science.howstuffworks.com.

9   Mary Nutting and Dave Nutting, "Families Are God's Idea,
    Beginning in Genesis," Answers in Genesis, last modified January
    13, 2018, https://answersingenesis.org.

10 "How Does the Bible Define a Good Christian Family?" Got
    Questions Ministries, accessed March 5, 2020, https://www.
    gotquestions.org.

11 Michael G. Rogers, "Employee Conflict: Personal Story: 3 Important Leadership Tips," Teamwork and Leadership, accessed March 4, 2020, https://www.teamworkandleadership.com.

12 Morgan Cutolo, "This Fast-food Chain Has the Best Customer Service in America," Trusted Media Brands, Inc., last modified January 29, 2020, https://www.rd.com.

13 Jason Chatraw, "Flipping a Crackhouse," The Brink, February 18, 2020, http://thebrinkonline.com.

14 Marcel Schwantes, "9 Ways to Get Rid of Workplace Gossip Immediately," Inc.com, January 25, 2017, https://www.inc.com.

15 Rev. Manson B. Johnson, "Men God Chooses for His Greatness," Houston Forward Times, July 18, 2018, http://forwardtimes.com.

16 *Braveheart*, directed by Mel Gibson (1995; Hollywood, CA: Paramount Pictures 2000), DVD, 178 min.

17 Mel Chante, "Why Writing Down Your Vision is Powerful," December 12, 2017, http://melysalatham.com.

18 Mary Kay Ash, *You Can Have It All: Lifetime Wisdom from America's Foremost Woman Entrepreneur* (ed. Prima Lifestyles, 1995).

19 Charles Colson and Nancy Pearcey, *How Now Shall We Live?* (Illinois: Tyndale House Publishers, 1999), 33.

20 A.J. Jacobs, "Be a Pilgrim for a Day," AMG/Parade, November 15, 2009, https://parade.com.

21 John W. Kennedy, "Return on Investment," The General Council of the Assemblies of God, May 22, 2017, https://news.ag.org.

ABOUT THE AUTHOR

Os Hillman is an internationally recognized speaker, author, and consultant on the subject of faith in the workplace. Hillman has written twenty books on faith and work-related subjects and a daily workplace email devotional entitled *TGIF - Today God Is First* that is read by several hundred thousand people daily in 105 countries. He has been featured on CNBC, NBC, *The Los Angeles Times*, *The New York Times*, *The Associated Press,* and many other national media as a spokesperson on faith in the workplace. Os is founder and president of Marketplace Leaders, an organization designed to equip men and women to live out their calling in and through the marketplace, and through this ministry, he has equipped leaders in twenty-six countries. Os is married to Pamela, and they live in north Atlanta. Os has one daughter, Charis, married to Justin. To contact Os Hillman, send your email to os@marketplaceleaders.org.

More Books by Os Hillman

*Overcoming Hindrances to
Fulfilling Your Destiny*

Listening to the Father's Heart

Experiencing the Father's Love

*The Upside of Adversity: Rising
From the Pit to Greatness*

*Change Agent: Engaging Your
Passion to Be the One
Who Makes a Difference*

*The 9 to 5 Window: How Faith
Can Transform the Workplace*

The Purposes of Money

Faith & Work: Do They Mix?

*Faith@Work Movement:
What Every Pastor and Church
Leader Should Know*

*How to Discover Why God Made
You (Booklet)*

*TGIF paperback 270 devotionals
by topic*

TGIF (Pocket Version)

TGIF Volume 2

TGIF Small Group Bible Study

*The Joseph Calling: 6 Stages
to Discover, Navigate,
and Fulfill Your Purpose*

*The Joseph Calling
12-week Bible study*

*Proven Strategies for
Business Success*

So You Want to Write a Book

Are You a Biblical Worker?

To order
TGIFBookstore.com
678.455.6262 x103
info@marketplaceleaders.org

Let's continue the
conversation.
Join other workplace leaders
in our Change Agent
MasterMentor Program.

Learn more at
CAMasterMentorProgram.
com

Websites
TodayGodIsFirst.com
TheChangeAgentNetwork.
com
MarketplaceLeaders.org
TGIFBookstore.com
CultureShapersNetwork.org

Download our free app,
TGIF Os Hillman,
via Google Play
or iTunes App Store.

BroadStreet Publishing® Group, LLC
Savage, Minnesota, USA
BroadStreetPublishing.com

31 DECREES OF BLESSING FOR YOUR WORK LIFE
Copyright © 2021 Os Hillman

978-1-4245-6107-0 (faux leather)
978-1-4245-6108-7 (e-book)

Stock or custom editions of BroadStreet Publishing titles may be purchased in bulk for educational, business, ministry, fundraising, or sales promotional use. For information, please email orders@broadstreetpublishing.com.

Cover and interior by Garborg Design at GarborgDesign.com

Printed in China

21 22 23 24 25 5 4 3 2 1